Winning at College Campus Interviews

(Making that IMPACT!)

Gerard Assey

Winning at College Campus Interviews

By

Gerard Assey

Published by:
Gerard Assey
19/18, Palli Arasan Street
Anna Nagar East
Chennai - 600 102

ISBN: 978-81-967202-7-8

(Image by macrovector on Freepik 'https://www.freepik.com' Thank You)

Table of Contents

Preface

Welcome to '***Winning at College Campus Interviews,'*** a comprehensive guide designed to empower you, the college graduate, in navigating the challenging yet rewarding transition from academic life to the professional world. As you stand on the threshold of your career, this book aims to be your trusted companion, providing insights, strategies, and practical advice to help you not just survive but thrive in the competitive landscape of campus interviews.

The journey from college to the corporate realm is an exciting adventure, brimming with opportunities, challenges, and moments of self-discovery. We understand the significance of this pivotal phase in your life, and this guide has been meticulously crafted to serve as a roadmap, offering guidance through the intricacies of the interview process.

Our goal is to equip you with the knowledge and tools needed to not only excel in interviews but to also cultivate a mindset of continuous learning and improvement. This book addresses every facet of the interview journey, from understanding the purpose of interviews and effective preparation to handling various interview formats, building rapport, and making informed decisions post-interview.

Drawing from real-world experiences, industry insights, and best practices, "Winning at College Campus Interviews" is not just a theoretical guide but a practical resource that reflects the dynamic nature of the professional landscape. The content is presented in a reader-friendly manner, avoiding jargon and embracing a conversational tone to ensure accessibility and engagement.

As you immerse yourself in these pages, you'll discover strategies for effective communication, learn how to handle behavioral and competency-based questions, and gain insights into the nuances of sending impactful thank-you notes. Each chapter is a step towards honing your skills, boosting your confidence, and ultimately positioning yourself as a standout candidate in the eyes of prospective employers.

This guide is not a one-size-fits-all solution but a versatile toolkit designed to cater to your unique strengths, aspirations, and challenges. It encourages you to embrace the journey, acknowledging that every interview is an opportunity for growth and refinement. Your success is not just measured by the job offer you secure but by the lessons you learn, the connections you make, and the continuous evolution of your professional identity.

Whether you are preparing for your first-ever interview or seeking to enhance your existing skills, "Winning at College Campus Interviews" is here to support you. We believe in your potential, and with the right mindset and preparation, you can emerge victorious in this transformative chapter of your life.

Best wishes on your journey from the academic halls to the corporate corridors. May this guide serve as a beacon of guidance, inspiration, and practical wisdom as you navigate the exciting world of campus interviews.

Navigating 'Winning at College Campus Interviews'

This chapter is designed to guide you on how to effectively utilize this book to enhance your interview preparation and maximize your success in securing a job after graduation. Let's embark on a step-by-step journey through the contents and structure of this comprehensive guide.

Step 1: Orientation

Start with the Preface

Begin your journey by reading the Preface. Understand the motivation behind this guide, the author's perspective, and the commitment to providing you with practical insights. This will set the tone for your exploration of the subsequent chapters.

Step 2: Overview of Contents

Familiarize Yourself with the Table of Contents

Take a moment to review the Table of Contents. This will give you a bird's-eye view of the topics covered, allowing you to identify areas of immediate relevance and those you may want to explore later.

Step 3: Structured Reading

Follow the Order of Chapters

Read the chapters sequentially. The content is structured in a logical flow, starting from understanding interviews to handling various interview types, effective preparation, and concluding with post-interview strategies. This sequence ensures a progressive and comprehensive learning experience.

Step 4: Active Engagement

Reflect on Your Own Experiences

As you read, reflect on your own experiences. Relate the concepts to your academic background, personal strengths, and career aspirations. Consider how the insights provided can be applied to your unique situation.

Step 5: Practical Application

Utilize Action Plans and Templates

The guide includes action plans, examples, and templates to make the content actionable. Apply the suggested strategies, practice with the templates provided, and customize them to suit your individual style.

Step 6: Personal Reflection

Use the Reflection Sections

At the end of each chapter, find the personal reflection sections. Take time to internalize the key takeaways, jot down your thoughts, and consider how you can implement the lessons learned in your own interview preparations.

Step 7: Continuous Learning

Explore Additional Resources

This guide is a starting point, not the endpoint. Use the recommended resources and references to delve deeper into specific topics. Stay curious and continue learning beyond the scope of this book.

Step 8: Practical Exercises

Engage with Practical Exercises

Several chapters include practical exercises to reinforce your understanding. Engage with these exercises actively to enhance your interview skills. Consider recording mock interviews, practicing responses, and seeking feedback.

Step 9: Post-Chapter Actions

Implement Action Items

At the end of each chapter, find actionable steps and recommendations. Implement these suggestions in your interview preparation. This could include refining your resume, practicing specific interview scenarios, or enhancing your online presence.

Step 10: Utilize the Conclusion

Draw Inspiration from the Conclusion

In the conclusion, find inspiration and encouragement. Use the provided template for personal reflection to consolidate your thoughts on your journey from college to the professional world.

Step 11: Continuous Improvement

Embrace Continuous Learning

Remember, success in interviews is not just about mastering a set of skills; it's about embracing a mindset of continuous improvement. Every interview is an opportunity to learn, adapt, and grow.

As you navigate "Winning at College Campus Interviews," approach it as a dynamic tool for your professional development. Tailor the strategies to your unique situation, engage actively with the content, and view each chapter as a building block toward your success in campus interviews.

May this guide serve as a valuable resource on your journey from college graduate to a confident and successful job candidate. Best of luck!

Importance of Campus Interviews

Securing a job after graduation is a pivotal step in the journey towards a successful career. One of the crucial milestones in this process is the campus interview. This chapter provides a comprehensive guide to help graduates not only navigate but excel in campus interviews, ensuring they emerge victorious in the competitive corporate world.

The importance of campus interviews cannot be overstated. These interviews serve as a bridge between the academic world and the professional arena, offering graduates the opportunity to showcase their skills and potential to potential employers. A successful campus interview can open doors to promising career paths, making it a critical aspect of the transition from student life to the corporate landscape.

Setting the Tone:

As we embark on this journey together, it's essential to recognize that the path from being a graduate to a successful job candidate is multifaceted. It involves not only possessing the right skills and knowledge but also mastering the art of presenting oneself effectively during interviews. This book aims to be your guide, providing insights, strategies, and practical tips to empower you to approach campus interviews with confidence and competence.

Throughout the chapters that follow, we will delve into various aspects of interview preparation, covering everything from understanding the purpose of interviews to handling different interview types, mastering effective communication, and ultimately securing the job offer. Each section is crafted to equip you with the tools needed to navigate the complexities of the interview process successfully.

Consider this book as your companion on this transformative journey. By the end, you'll not only understand the intricacies of campus interviews but also be well-prepared to demonstrate your value to potential employers. Let's embark on this adventure together, and may your campus interviews become stepping stones to a fulfilling and rewarding professional career.

An Overview of Interviews

Interviews play a pivotal role in the hiring process, acting as a critical bridge between the candidate's academic achievements and their potential contributions to a company. By comprehensively understanding the purpose of interviews and the stages of the selection process, candidates can navigate these interactions with confidence and strategy.

The Purpose of Interviews

Importance of Interviews in the Hiring Process:

Interviews serve as a dynamic platform for employers to evaluate candidates beyond their resumes. While academic achievements and qualifications are essential, interviews allow employers to gauge soft skills, communication abilities, and cultural fit. It's an opportunity for candidates to showcase their personality, enthusiasm, and suitability for the role.
Example: Imagine two candidates with identical academic backgrounds applying for a sales position. Through an interview, the employer can assess each candidate's interpersonal skills, understanding of client interactions, and ability to handle challenging situations, ultimately helping in making a more informed hiring decision.

How Interviews Help Employers Assess Candidates:

Interviews provide employers with valuable insights into a candidate's problem-solving skills, adaptability, and interpersonal dynamics. By engaging in a face-to-face or virtual conversation, employers can gauge

a candidate's reaction to unexpected scenarios, assess their thought processes, and evaluate their potential cultural alignment with the organization.
Example: In a project management role, an employer might ask a candidate about a challenging situation they faced in a previous role and how they resolved it. The response not only showcases the candidate's problem-solving abilities but also provides a glimpse into their decision-making process under pressure.

Understanding the Stages of the Selection Process

Overview of the Entire Hiring Process:

The hiring process is a multifaceted journey, encompassing various stages from application submission to final job offer. Understanding this journey is crucial for candidates to tailor their approach at each stage, increasing the likelihood of success.
Example: A typical hiring process may include resume screening, initial interviews, assessments, a final interview, and reference checks. Each stage is designed to narrow down the candidate pool, with the final interview serving as the last step before a job offer.

Importance of Each Stage in the Selection Process:

Each stage of the selection process serves a specific purpose. From resume screening to the final interview, employers progressively gather information about candidates, ensuring a comprehensive evaluation before extending a job offer.
Example: During the initial stages, employers may focus on assessing basic qualifications and skills. As

candidates progress through subsequent stages, the focus shifts to more in-depth evaluations, such as behavioral assessments and scenario-based interviews, ensuring a holistic understanding of their capabilities.

Types of Interviews and Tips for Each Type

Traditional One-on-One Interviews:

Traditional interviews involve a one-on-one conversation between the candidate and an interviewer. Success in these interviews hinges on effective communication, showcasing relevant skills, and building a connection with the interviewer.

Action Plan: Practice answering common questions while maintaining eye contact, expressing enthusiasm, and tailoring responses to highlight your strengths.

Panel Interviews:

Panel interviews involve multiple interviewers assessing a candidate simultaneously. Navigating panel interviews requires adaptability, as candidates must engage with each panel member while conveying a consistent and compelling narrative.

Template: Prepare a brief introduction that covers your academic background, key skills, and career aspirations. Use this as a foundation to answer questions from various panel members while maintaining coherence and relevance.

Behavioral Interviews:

Behavioral interviews focus on past behaviors as indicators of future performance. Candidates are asked to provide specific examples of how they handled situations in the past, highlighting key competencies.

Action Plan: Develop a repository of anecdotes that showcase your problem-solving abilities, teamwork, leadership, and resilience. Structure responses using the STAR (Situation, Task, Action, Result) method for clarity.

Case Interviews:

Case interviews assess a candidate's analytical and problem-solving skills. Candidates are presented with a real or hypothetical business scenario and are required to analyze and propose solutions.

Example: If interviewing for a consulting role, a case interview might involve analyzing a client's business challenge and presenting a structured approach to address it.

Group Interviews:

Group interviews involve multiple candidates interacting in a collaborative setting. Success requires a balance between asserting individual contributions and demonstrating teamwork.

Tips: Observe active listening, contribute meaningfully to discussions, and acknowledge others' perspectives. This showcases your ability to work effectively in a group setting.

Phone and Video Interviews:

Phone and video interviews present unique challenges, including the absence of physical cues. Effective preparation involves mastering virtual communication and creating a professional virtual presence.

Action Plan: Ensure a quiet and well-lit space for video interviews. Test audio and video equipment beforehand to avoid technical glitches. Maintain good posture and engage with the interviewer through virtual eye contact.

Tips and Strategies for Success in Each Type of Interview:

Regardless of the interview type, certain universal strategies contribute to success. These include thorough research, effective communication, and the ability to articulate your unique value proposition.

Strategy: Tailor your responses to align with the company's values and mission. Showcase how your skills and experiences uniquely position you as an asset to the organization.

Research, Prepare, Practice

Importance of Research in Understanding the Company and Role:

Research serves as the foundation for effective interview preparation. By understanding the company's history, values, and current initiatives, candidates can tailor their responses to align with the organization's goals.

Action Plan: Visit the company's website, review recent press releases, and follow their social media channels. Take note of key projects, corporate culture, and any recent awards or achievements.

Tips for Effective Interview Preparation:

Effective interview preparation involves a combination of self-reflection, researching common interview questions, and practicing responses. This proactive approach enhances confidence and ensures a polished interview performance.

Action Plan: Create a list of potential interview questions and draft thoughtful responses. Practice delivering these responses aloud to refine your articulation and coherence.

Role of Practice in Building Confidence:
Practice is a fundamental element in interview success. It not only helps in refining responses but also enhances overall confidence and composure during the actual interview.
Action Plan: Engage in mock interviews with friends, family, or career advisors. Seek constructive feedback on your communication style, body language, and overall presentation.

In summary, understanding interviews involves recognizing their purpose, navigating the stages of the selection process, and mastering the various interview types. By investing time in research, preparation, and practice, candidates can position themselves as standout contenders, increasing their chances of success in the competitive job market. The subsequent chapters will delve deeper into each aspect, providing actionable insights and practical advice to empower you on your journey from graduate to successful job candidate.

Effective Interview Preparation

1. Before the Interview

Researching the Company and Role

Conducting thorough research about the company and the specific role is the cornerstone of effective interview preparation. This goes beyond just browsing the company's website; it involves understanding its culture, values, recent achievements, and even the challenges it might be facing.

Example: Suppose you're interviewing with a technology company. Researching recent product launches, market positioning, and any notable collaborations can provide valuable insights. Understanding the company's mission statement and values allows you to align your responses with their organizational culture during the interview.

Action Plan:

- ✓ Explore the company's official website, paying attention to mission statements, values, and leadership profiles.
- ✓ Read recent press releases, news articles, and industry reports related to the company.
- ✓ Connect with current or former employees on professional networking platforms like LinkedIn to gain insider perspectives.

What Areas to look into when Researching the Organization and Position: The interview is an opportunity for you to demonstrate your research skills to an employer. It is therefore important to find out as much as you can about the organization, with which you are interviewing. Learn as much about the organization:

- ✓ Location(s), size, products or services
- ✓ History, vision, mission statement and/or stated values
- ✓ Clients, competitors, collaborators
- ✓ Challenges, projects and successes
- ✓ Internal structure, leadership, policies, culture/climate
- ✓ Recent news and current projects
- ✓ What is the organization known for? Its goodwill and credibility in the market?
- ✓ What are the geographical locations of its plants, stores, or sales outlets?
- ✓ How well is the organization doing? (growth patterns)
- ✓ What is its organizational structure?
- ✓ Who are the organization's officers, administrators, etc.? Know something of their background and recent achievements.
- ✓ Analyze the job description and how your background, skills, and experience apply to the position. Evaluate your interest in this career field and be able to verbalize it. If the job description is limited, research similar jobs in similar companies
- ✓ How much potential for advancement is there within this structure?
- ✓ Find out how the position you are applying for relates to the whole organization. Try to pinpoint some challenges, opportunities, policies, or philosophies of the organization, and plan to speak knowledgeably about these during the interview.

- ✓ Don't be surprised if one of the first questions interviewers ask when you arrive is, *"Have you have had a chance to look at our website"?*

Customizing Your Resume and Portfolio (Complete details in a later chapter)
Tailoring your resume and portfolio to align with the specific requirements of the job demonstrates a thoughtful and personalized approach. Highlighting relevant experiences, skills, and accomplishments can make a significant impact on how well you fit the role.

Template: Use a targeted resume template that emphasizes key skills and experiences relevant to the job description. Include quantifiable achievements to provide concrete evidence of your capabilities.

Action Plan:

- ✓ Analyze the job description and identify key skills and qualifications.
- ✓ Customize your resume to emphasize experiences that directly align with the job requirements.
- ✓ Create a portfolio showcasing relevant projects, presentations, or work samples that demonstrate your skills.

Setting Up a Professional Online Presence
In the digital age, your online presence is often the first impression you make on potential employers. Ensuring a professional and consistent image across various online platforms is crucial.

Action Plan:

- ✓ Update your LinkedIn profile with a professional photo, comprehensive work history, and a well-crafted headline.
- ✓ Google yourself to identify any potentially unprofessional content and take steps to address it.
- ✓ Consider creating a personal website to showcase your portfolio, achievements, and a blog highlighting your industry insights.

2. Day of Interview

Dressing for Success

Your attire is a non-verbal expression of your professionalism and respect for the opportunity. Dressing appropriately contributes to creating a positive first impression.

Action Plan:

- ✓ Research the company's dress code and choose an outfit that aligns with their culture.
- ✓ Ensure your clothes are clean, well-fitted, and in good condition.
- ✓ Pay attention to grooming and avoid excessive accessories or clothing that may be distracting.

Creating an Excellent First Impression

The first few minutes of an interview are critical in shaping the overall perception of the candidate. Establishing a positive and memorable first impression sets the tone for the entire interview.

Action Plan:

- ✓ Practice a firm and confident handshake.
- ✓ Maintain good eye contact and offer a genuine smile.

- ✓ Introduce yourself with a concise and compelling elevator pitch that highlights your key strengths and experiences.

Handling Nerves and Anxiety

Feeling nervous before an interview is natural, but effective strategies can help manage anxiety and promote a calm, collected demeanor.

Action Plan:

- ✓ Practice mindfulness techniques, such as deep breathing or visualization, to calm nerves.
- ✓ Engage in a pre-interview routine that includes positive affirmations and a brief review of key talking points.
- ✓ Remind yourself that interviews are opportunities to showcase your skills and experiences, not tests of personal worth.

Tips for Punctuality

Being punctual demonstrates professionalism and respect for others' time. Arriving late can create a negative impression, regardless of your qualifications.

Action Plan:

- ✓ Plan your route to the interview location, considering potential traffic or public transportation delays.
- ✓ Aim to arrive 15-20 minutes early, allowing time for unexpected issues.
- ✓ Carry contact information for the interviewer in case of unforeseen circumstances.

3. After the Interview

Sending Thank-You Notes

A well-crafted thank-you note is a courteous gesture that reinforces your interest in the position and leaves a positive impression.

Template:

Dear [Interviewer's Name],

I wanted to express my gratitude for the opportunity to interview with [Company Name]. It was a pleasure discussing [specific aspects of the interview or the role], and I am excited about the prospect of contributing to [Company's goals]. Thank you for your time, and I look forward to the possibility of joining your team.

Sincerely,

[Your Full Name]

Action Plan:

- ✓ Send personalized thank-you emails within 24 hours of the interview.
- ✓ Mention specific aspects of the interview or discussions to show genuine interest.
- ✓ Reiterate your enthusiasm for the position and the company.

Assessing Your Performance

Reflecting on your interview performance helps identify strengths and areas for improvement. Honest self-assessment is crucial for continuous growth.

Action Plan:

- ✓ Review your responses and the overall flow of the interview.
- ✓ Identify moments where you effectively communicated your skills and experiences.
- ✓ Take note of areas where you can refine your responses or provide more impactful examples.

Strategies for Continuous Improvement

Every interview experience is a learning opportunity. Developing a mindset of continuous improvement ensures you refine your approach based on feedback and experiences.

Action Plan:

- ✓ Seek feedback from mentors, career advisors, or peers who can provide constructive insights.
- ✓ Keep a record of common interview questions and your responses for future reference.
- ✓ Stay updated on industry trends and incorporate relevant information into your responses.

In conclusion, effective interview preparation involves comprehensive research, personalized customization of application materials, professional online presence, meticulous attention to the day-of interview details, and a strategic approach to post-interview actions. These elements collectively contribute to a candidate's success in navigating the competitive landscape of campus interviews. The subsequent chapters will build upon these foundational principles, offering deeper insights and actionable strategies for specific interview scenarios and challenges.

Preparing Self

Creating an Excellent First Impression
Importance of Body Language and Appearance
The impact of a first impression cannot be overstated, and body language plays a crucial role in shaping perceptions during interviews. Non-verbal cues, such as posture, facial expressions, and gestures, contribute significantly to how you are perceived.
Example: Imagine a candidate entering the interview room with slouched shoulders and avoiding eye contact. Despite having an impressive resume, the candidate's body language may convey a lack of confidence or disinterest. Conversely, a candidate with an upright posture, a firm handshake, and positive facial expressions communicates professionalism and enthusiasm.
Action Plan:

- ✓ Maintain Good Posture: Sit or stand up straight to convey confidence and attentiveness.
- ✓ Eye Contact: Establish and maintain eye contact to show sincerity and engagement.
- ✓ Facial Expressions: Smile appropriately and express interest through your facial expressions.
- ✓ Gestures: Use purposeful gestures to emphasize points, but avoid distracting or nervous movements.

The Handshake/Greeting Do's & Don'ts
The handshake and initial greeting set the tone for the interview. A confident and appropriate

handshake can establish a positive rapport, while an awkward or weak handshake may create a negative impression.

Action Plan:

Do's:

- ✓ Offer a firm handshake, matching the grip strength of the other person.
- ✓ Accompany the handshake with a warm and genuine smile.
- ✓ Maintain eye contact during the greeting.

Don'ts:

- ✓ Avoid a limp or overly aggressive handshake.
- ✓ Steer clear of excessive hand movements or gestures during the handshake.
- ✓ Refrain from looking down or away during the greeting.

Dealing with Nerves

Techniques for Managing Anxiety

Nervousness before an interview is natural, and managing anxiety is essential for delivering a confident and composed performance. Employing effective techniques can help calm nerves and enhance your overall interview experience.

Example: Consider a candidate experiencing interview anxiety. By employing relaxation techniques, such as deep breathing or progressive muscle relaxation, the candidate can alleviate tension, allowing for clearer thinking and improved communication during the interview.

Action Plan:

- ✓ Deep Breathing: Practice deep breathing exercises to calm your nerves. Inhale deeply through your nose, hold for a few seconds, and exhale slowly through your mouth.

- ✓ Visualization: Visualize a successful interview scenario, envisioning yourself confidently answering questions and engaging with the interviewer.
- ✓ Progressive Muscle Relaxation: Tense and then gradually release different muscle groups to alleviate physical tension associated with nervousness.

Preparing for Tasks

Presentations, Group Discussions, Delivering a Lesson, Solving a Case Study, etc.

Different interviews may involve various tasks, such as presentations, group discussions, or solving case studies. Effective preparation for these tasks requires a combination of knowledge, communication skills, and strategic planning.

Example: If an interview involves a case study presentation, a candidate must not only understand the problem but also communicate a structured analysis and propose solutions. Practice in advance ensures a confident and articulate delivery.

Action Plan:

- ✓ Research the Task: Understand the specific requirements of the task, whether it's a presentation, group discussion, or case study.
- ✓ Structured Approach: Develop a structured approach to tasks, ensuring clarity in your presentation or discussion.
- ✓ Practice Sessions: Rehearse your presentation or discussion with a friend or mentor to receive constructive feedback.
- ✓ Time Management: Practice time management to ensure that you can

effectively cover all aspects of the task within the allotted time.

Using a Mind Map to Brainstorm Current Developments in Your Field of Study

A mind map is a visual tool that can aid in brainstorming and organizing information. Using a mind map to prepare for current developments in your field of study helps in presenting comprehensive and organized responses during interviews.

Action Plan:

- ✓ Central Topic: Identify the central theme or topic related to your field of study.
- ✓ Branch Out: Create branches for key subtopics or categories, such as recent trends, innovations, or challenges.
- ✓ Add Details: Under each subtopic, add specific details, facts, or examples that demonstrate your knowledge.
- ✓ Review and Refine: Periodically review and refine your mind map to stay updated on the latest developments.

An Example of using a Mind Map to Brainstorm Current Developments in your Field of Study.

For this illustration, let's assume you are a recent graduate in computer science interested in artificial intelligence (AI). Here's how you can structure your mind map:

Using a Mind Map to Brainstorm Current Developments in AI (Computer Science)

Central Idea: Artificial Intelligence in Computer Science

Start your mind map with the central idea in the middle, representing the broad topic – in this case, AI in computer science.

Major Branches: Categories of AI

Create major branches representing categories or aspects of AI that you want to explore. For example:

- ✓ Machine Learning
- ✓ Natural Language Processing
- ✓ Computer Vision
- ✓ Robotics

Sub-Branches: Specific Developments

Under each major branch, add sub-branches to highlight specific developments or trends. For instance:

- ✓ *Machine Learning*
- ✓ Deep Learning Advancements
- ✓ Transfer Learning Applications
- ✓ Reinforcement Learning in AI
- ✓ *Natural Language Processing*
- ✓ Advances in Conversational AI
- ✓ Sentiment Analysis Breakthroughs
- ✓ Multilingual NLP Models
- ✓ *Computer Vision*
- ✓ Object Detection Improvements
- ✓ Image Recognition Breakthroughs
- ✓ AI in Medical Imaging
- ✓ *Robotics*
- ✓ Collaborative Robotics
- ✓ AI-Powered Autonomous Robots
- ✓ Human-Robot Interaction

Key Players and Projects

Extend your mind map to include key players and notable projects in each sub-branch. For example:

- ✓ *Deep Learning Advancements*
- ✓ Notable Projects: AlphaGo, GPT-3

- ✓ Key Players: OpenAI, Google Brain
- ✓ *Object Detection Improvements*
- ✓ Notable Projects: YOLO, Faster R-CNN
- ✓ Key Players: Facebook AI Research, Microsoft Research

Impact and Applications

Consider the impact of each development and its real-world applications:

- ✓ *Reinforcement Learning in AI*
- ✓ Impact: Advancements in autonomous systems.
- ✓ Applications: Self-driving cars, game playing, robotics.

Global Trends and Challenges

Explore global trends and challenges associated with these developments:

- ✓ *Multilingual NLP Models*
- ✓ Trend: Growing demand for language-agnostic models.
- ✓ Challenge: Addressing bias and ethical considerations.

Utilizing the Mind Map for Interview Preparation

During an interview, you can use this mind map to:

Showcase Awareness: Discuss recent developments in the chosen categories to demonstrate your up-to-date knowledge.

- ✓ Highlight Expertise: Emphasize your expertise in specific areas, providing examples of projects or advancements you find particularly intriguing.
- ✓ Connect Developments: Draw connections between different branches, showcasing a holistic understanding of AI in computer science.

- ✓ Discuss Implications: Explore the potential impact of these developments on the industry and society at large.

Remember, the goal is not to memorize every detail but to have a well-organized mental map that allows you to navigate through the latest trends and advancements in your field with confidence during an interview.

In summary, preparing oneself for an interview involves mastering the art of creating an excellent first impression, managing nerves effectively, and readying oneself for various interview tasks. By understanding the significance of body language, perfecting the handshake, employing anxiety management techniques, and strategically preparing for specific tasks, candidates can enhance their overall performance during interviews. These elements collectively contribute to a candidate's self-assurance and ability to showcase their skills and qualifications effectively. The subsequent chapters will build upon these foundational principles, offering deeper insights into specific interview scenarios and advanced preparation strategies.

Your Attitude is Most Important!

In any environment, whether at home or at work, the tendency to think positively and approach each and every task with a "can-do" attitude can be really infectious. Organizations are therefore very careful to hire the right kinds of people to prevent any potential problems among existing employees, as when it comes to collaborating on projects, or in a team, the positive attitude can spill over into the way employees cooperate with one another. On the other hand, employees with a poor attitude about work and the tasks they are required to complete will have a negative effect on those around them. Just as a positive attitude is infectious and spreads to others, so too will poor attitudes have a negative effect on employee relations, resulting in division in the workplace, making it difficult for employees to collaborate with one another, as the poor attitudes spill over into how they treat one another.

If you are a student, job seeker, business person or are planning to get into business, or are working for a business, you will know that while every business requires C.A.S.H. to survive and succeed....Every Professional also needs something to succeed, which I believe is more valuable than the CASH that comes in.

This is 'K.A.S.H.' because only when you have this KASH in you, you will be more successful in bringing in the CASH for you and/or the organization you represent, by ensuring and protecting the credibility and image of the organization

So what is this KASH?

- ✓ **K**nowledge
- ✓ **A**ttitude
- ✓ **S**kills
- ✓ **H**abits

Knowledge is all about a Company's Products or Services that they offer, the Market and Industry/domain that they operate in, together with knowing of who are the other players or the competition that are in this industry. It also involves knowing where the organization stand against them-their strengths and areas that the competition has an advantage over, along with being thorough on the rates, polices and regulations in the industry and market.

How effectively are you able to transfer any knowledge you possess, to the customer/ others to enable them to deal or decide upon the next step or you as their service provider is a skill.

Now there are various types of skill sets that people possess-Some examples for skills are:

Interpersonal Skills
Computer Programming Skills
Problem Solving Skills
Selling Skills
Networking Skills
Time Management
Team Working
Presentation Skills
Effective Probing Skills
Ability to present thoughts/ product demos
Effective Communication Skills
People Handing Skills/ Inter-personal Skills
Content Writing Skills etc

Now having just Knowledge and Skills alone is not enough. There are many people you probably know of that have a great bank of knowledge along with the necessary skills, but yet have been total failures. Reason being they had a lousy attitude or very poor habits that killed a potential sale or the potential in them; that ultimately affected theirs and their organizations credibility

What you are seeing on the pie chart is the mental make-up of a Professional. As you will see, 50% has to do with the Attitude, followed by 25% on People Skills. In other words, if you don't have the required knowledge or skills, as you can see, you may be able to still succeed with the right attitude and people skills, because those two account for 75%. Now don't get me wrong, I am not saying that you should not work on your knowledge and skills…Absolutely no!

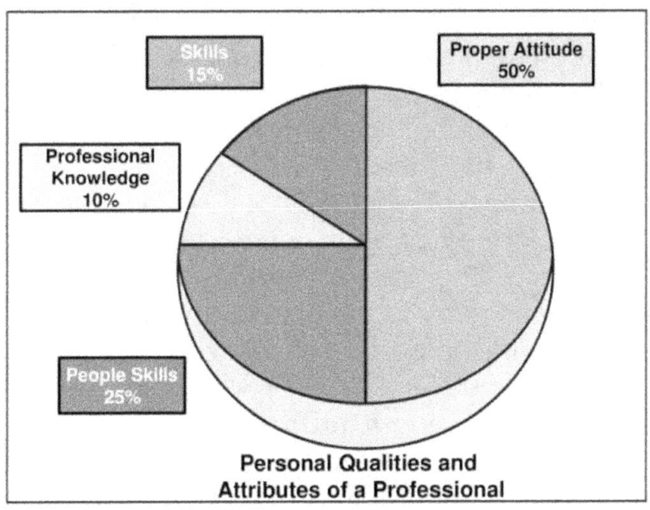

What I am saying is that given that you have the right attitude coupled with the right people skills, knowledge and skills, you don't have to guess where your career graph would be!

Let us look at this a little differently….Assuming you have the right attitude and people skills, which together comprise of 75% but lack the required knowledge and skills, well then, to me, with the right attitude you can easily learn them. And one of the attributes potential employers look for in candidates is someone who has a desire to learn or is teachable, as Knowledge and Skills are teachable, but not Attitude!

Attitude is the outlook or perception towards a given situation, and for any professional, this is extremely crucial and foundational! Attitude is made up from our upbringing, environment, exposure etc. It would therefore be very difficult or it would take a long time to undo a wrong attitude that has gone in all these years. And if you are working with people, like that of a sales or customer service professional, or in the hospitality field, then this is very important- as customers remember the wrong or negative attitude longer. You are the only thing the customer sometimes sees of your company- and this is the impression formed of your entire company- good or bad! It takes a long time to undo this negative feeling about your company in the mind of the customer.

At this stage it is important to realize that there are **3 A's of Business life**:

Ability, Ambition and **Attitude**

- ✓ Ability establishes 'what' someone does
- ✓ Ambition determines 'how much' he does
- ✓ But Attitude alone 'guarantees how' he does it!

Ability will bring one a pay cheque (check)
Ambition will get him a raise
Attitude alone will lead to success in everything!

Attitude is actually the 'YOU on the job. When ability and ambition in two people are about equal, how does the boss select one over the other for promotion? Here is where Attitude is the deciding factor. Attitude reflects a little plus- that something extra is given willingly though not required.

If you look at the word A-T-T-I-T-U-D-E itself, is it a mere coincidence that "I" comes first and "U" later? If this has any significance, then in trying to understand the attitudes of people, we should first examine ourselves in relation to other people!

Because Attitude is so very important, this is why it is so crucial to fill our minds with the right positive thoughts because our thoughts work into decisions that form our actions and this continued action leads to a habit, which eventually makes up our attitude. Your habits today will become your attitude in the days to come. That's why it is important to check our habits as well. As an example: The habit of being late (at say your office), if not nipped in the early stages can lead it to becoming an attitude, with everything that you undertake being late or delayed!

Here are some examples of positive or right attitude:

Belief
Commitment
Desire
Ability to fail & learn from it
Persistent goals
Self-Motivation
Enthusiasm
Purpose

Self-discipline
Confidence
Creativity
Empathy
Go the extra mile
Self-improvement
Time organization
...and most of all the *PASSION!*

Great Professionals...

- ✓ Understand themselves and how their behavior affects others
- ✓ Have a positive attitude, which reflects in dedication to getting it right the first time, and commitment to helping others
- ✓ Know how to adapt their behavior to meet the differing needs of the situation
- ✓ A willingness to take responsibility
- ✓ Have the confidence to stay calm under pressure

Attitude Impacts Outcome

Steps to change your Attitude...

- ✓ Become aware of your negative attitude towards yourself, other people and situations and alter your thinking
- ✓ Think for yourself and become more constructive
- ✓ Keep an open mind

Remember: Changes are always: M.A.D.E...!!!

Developing GREAT Positive Attitudes is not something that happens to you-it is something you make happen...and like any change, it is not easy!

Here are some steps that can help:

M- Mental Pictures: Visualize who you are, what you want, how will you conduct and carry yourself

A- Affirmations: Add a new self-image by talking positively
D- Daily Successes: Build confidence everyday by looking at your positives rather than negatives
E- Environmental Influences: Surround yourself with positive influencers, read positive stuff, listen and watch positive information etc

You are what you think! To change any habits, you must first change any thoughts, feelings and values!

Changing Bad Habits into Good Ones!

Step 1: List your bad habits
Step 2: What were the original causes?
Step 3: What are the supporting causes?
Step 4: Determine a positive habit to replace the bad one.
Step 5: Think about the good habit, its benefits and results.
Step 6: Take action to develop this habit.
Step 7: Daily act upon this habit for reinforcement.
Step 8: Reward yourself by noting one of the benefits from your good habit

Demonstrating the RIGHT Attitude …

There are three simple things you can do to be successful in your life and in your business:

- ✓ Smile
- ✓ Show Interest in other people
- ✓ Be a Candle- bring light into the lives around you

How to stand out from the crowd?

- ✓ Put your SIGNATURE on everything you do!
- ✓ Do it from your heart!

- ✓ It's not what you do that matters, but how much love you put in what you do that matters!
- ✓ GIVE 100%

Remember: Success is in YOUR Hands

As can be seen, PERSONAL QUALITY is the basis of all other quality and is instrumental in determining your own future as well as your organization's profitability and future!

Why Self-Esteem Matters too: How to Build a High Self-Esteem!

Self-esteem refers to a person's beliefs about their own worth and value- it reflects the "confidence in one's own worth or abilities" and is the single limiting factor in those who under-succeed. It also has to do with the feelings people experience that follows from their sense of worthiness or unworthiness. Self-esteem is important because it heavily influences people's choices and decisions- especially when interacting with one another.

While typically not a topic discussed, many professionals struggle with issues of low self-esteem. They question their abilities to cope with the problems at hand, they often doubt they are worthy of the position they occupy, and they most definitely agonize quietly over much of their professional existence.

People with high self-esteem are people who are motivated to take care of themselves and to persistently strive towards the fulfillment of personal goals and aspirations. People with lower self-esteem don't tend to regard themselves as worthy of happy outcomes or capable of achieving them and so tend to let important things slide and to be less persistent and resilient in terms of overcoming adversity.

So it is important to appreciate how low self-esteem can have a major impact on your daily interaction with others, if it is not at least basically understood and addressed.

An individual with high self-esteem is likely to build their network by having a positive, open and 'can do' attitude. Conversely, an individual with low self-esteem is likely to lack that belief in him/ herself to start with. They will convince themselves (and others) that they have little that would be of interest to others.

Confidence versus Self-Esteem

A lot has been said and published with a great debate on the subject of 'Confidence'. A lot of people want to be more confident, without knowing the actual meaning of it.

A few points to note about confidence is that; it is 'External' and it is 'Temporary'. When I say external- I mean that in most times it is <u>not</u> in your control- somebody else is most of the time controlling it. When I say it is temporary I believe that for a day our confidence levels fluctuate several times depending on situations, circumstances, the people and environment we are in. That is why we do not recommend that people aim at only confidence.

Here is an example of what I mean:

You come into the office in the morning in a good mood-upbeat and all excited with a set of appointments you have for the day. However, your boss calls you into his cabin and pulls you up for a complaint that has come in from a top customer. What happens to your confidence level...One that was upbeat, is now down depending on how hard he came upon you!

Later, that same evening, you have bagged a huge order from another customer and that same boss now praises you as one of his best performers. What happens now? You are on top of the world, all up beat and charged up again.

As you can see in a single day your confidence levels can vary and fluctuate, which means they are temporary. Most times it is the effect or impact of others that have changed that feeling. It is like someone having a remote control on your life and your moods that can change or impact it every now and then.

A better, permanent solution to this for you as a Professional is to work on having a High Self Esteem. Let us now look deeper at what is Self Esteem?

Simply put...It is how much you value or respect yourself! The more you value or respect yourself, then, when you do face such situations like the example we've just seen, you are able to stay above- your value if it is 100, stays 100 and does not change! You now know that your boss has pulled you up for something wrong that you had done- but that does not change your value- it still remains 100.

Building your Self Esteem

Say out loud:

"I am the Most Valuable Person at work".

"I am the Most Valuable Person at my work". (Repeat it)

It's true. You are the most valuable person. No one else can quite fill your shoes. No one else can be you. You bring your unique being to work every day. You bring with you your talents, your abilities, your knowledge, your skills, your personality, or just your plain know-how. You may not be using all of your abilities just yet. You may not be using them to the fullest. You may not even recognize how valuable a person you are.

Healthy Self Esteem, not narcissistic, self-indulgent, or arrogance means to appreciate the value of you as a unique human being with your own special talents and abilities.

The word "esteem" in Latin, means, *"to value highly"* It would be impossible to value another person without first feeling valuable for yourself. When you place value on your own work and efforts, you can begin to find value in the work of others.

The Self-Image: Highway to Success

Have you ever said to yourself the following?

'I can't imagine myself being successful'

'I would like to, but I don't have enough experience or the right education'

'I can't get ahead because I'm too short, overweight, not good looking, my parents are poor, etc'.

The truth is most people talk themselves into failure and dejection. The result is the Fear of Trying.

Most of us know of or have read about common, everyday people who have become uncommonly productive and successful in their work and careers; individuals who have overcome enormous outer obstacles and inner roadblocks to become great.

Yet many people can't imagine doing such things themselves. They say, "*Yes, he could do it or she's doing it, but I can't because of______________".*

They develop the habit of failure. And it takes two forms:

Failure Reinforcement-the habit of looking back at past problems

Failure Forecasting-the habit of imagining the worst in the future

Because they lack sufficient self-esteem to believe in the validity of their dreams and purposes in life, they don't prepare for their achievement, and therefore are going down a dead-end street.

No wonder so many people feel trapped. Failure becomes set in their self-images. Never put yourself down- the workplace is full of put-downs- Don't do it yourself!

Self Esteem Takes Practice

Believe in yourself, no matter how long it takes or how tough it may seem at times.

There was once a college professor whose wife had a hearing deficiency. In trying to invent a device to enhance her hearing, he created something more complex that he thought might be useful to the public. He traveled throughout the New England states trying to find venture capital to take his idea into production. But businessmen everywhere laughed at him. *"Ideas are a dime a dozen."* They said: *"The project is doomed to failure."* Thank goodness, Alexander Graham Bell had the self-esteem to hang in there even when his only reward was his belief in himself.

Often we put imaginary barriers in our paths when no such barriers actually exist. In the 1940s, the greatest physicist and aeronautical engineers believed that the sound barriers could not be broken-that everyone or anything would be shattered when it approached the speed of sound. One lone pilot, Chuck Yeager, didn't believe it. He didn't think there was such a thing as sound "barrier". And indeed, he flew right through it.

Your Formula for Building a High Self-Esteem

How much you like yourself is the core energy force that determines your personality.

All STAR Performers have a program or formula for building self-esteem.

Steps You Can Take To Feel Better:

1. Action precedes feeling. Act your way into feeling something. Action triggers emotion. The role of pretending- act happy!
2. Set clear goals, so you can feel like a winner. Establish a VICTORY LIST for all your accomplishments. Set income goals (the WHAT) and personal goals (the WHY)
3. Accept 100% responsibility. *"IF IT'S TO BE, IT'S UP TO ME."* Or *"IF IT'S ALL FOR ME, IT'S UP TO ME"*. No excuses, no blaming.
4. Commit yourself to excellence. LEARN TO BE THE BEST in whatever you do. Say to yourself: *'I'M THE BEST (and) I LOVE MY WORK'*
5. Mental Rehearsal: Visualize the outcomes you desire, especially before you go to sleep at night. See yourself as strong, confident and relaxed, and see your customers, colleagues and others responding positively.
6. Get yourself a small note pad. Every night write down at least 3 positive things you did for that day- (it could be as small as even helping a person cross the road). Forget the negatives. Most times we go to bed filling our minds with all the negatives that occurred during the day. Just reverse it now. Look at only the positives. At the end of the year, you would have over one thousand positive things about you. Do you need any else then to tell you?
7. Believe in yourself-FAITH! Believe in yourself, your company and your products.
8. INTEGRITY AND HONESTY. They are at the root of success in anything you do. Never expect to be successful without being willing to pay the price. Never expect the rewards without working. Don't look for shortcuts.

9. Have confident expectations. Look for the good in every situation. Expect the best.

10. Practice the Law of Increasing Returns-the more you give thanks, the more you will have thanks for.

Managing You:
Positive First Impressions!

Have you ever wondered about the impressions you could create even before you open our mouth?
In a study carried out that I am about to share with you now, you will notice that people place more emphasis on what they SEE rather than on what they HEAR. So this only tells us that we need to be very careful with our body language and what we are projecting.
According to studies carried out, Communication takes place in 3 forms:

- ✓ Your Words
- ✓ Your Tone and
- ✓ Your Body Language.

Where 55% has to do with your Body Language or what others 'See'
7 % has to do with 'What' you say or your words
Whilst 38% has to do with 'How' those words are said, which is your Tone or voice modulation
With people going by what they SEE first rather than what they HEAR, it makes it very important for us to therefore project the RIGHT image upfront. That's the first impression that has been formed-good or bad! If it is good, then very good for you, but if it is bad, then so sad! Because…now you have double work to undo the wrong impression that has already gone into the mind and to now fill it with the right impression.
They say 90% of lasting impressions are created in the first 90 seconds. That can be really dangerous, but surprisingly that is true! So we have to be very careful, with what are we projecting as soon as

someone sees us, because that's what they will remember.

It is also a reason why we tend to remember a song seen on a television set better than when heard through a radio. The same logic applies at a job interview with your resume and the presentation of it! Then at the interview-the interviewer has made up his mind to a great extent as you walk in, even before you have opened your mouth. Your resume or the interview process is only a confirmation of the decision already made in the mind of the interviewer.

Why is Tone next important after Body Language? Simply because you can say a same sentence with a different tone and that can change the entire meaning

Eg; "Mary come here" is a simple sentence. But depending on the right tone, this one sentence could turn out as an 'order 'or a 'request'.

Another stronger example: "Hang him not let him go"...could be death or life depending on how it is said. Example: 'Hang him, not let him go'! Or 'Hang him not, let him go'!

Now, if it is face to face, we may be able to save the situation, but when on the phone with the other person not able to see you, it could lead to miscommunication if the right tone is not used.

As seen earlier, with people going by what they 'See' first rather than what they 'Hear', it makes it so very important for us to therefore project the RIGHT image upfront. It basically involves Selling Yourself first!

Before a customer buys anything or decides to do business with you or the company that you represent, he needs to first be sold on you because you are what he sees about your company to him.

Your company could have a several floor building, with several offices all across the globe. But to the person doing business with you, what he sees in you is the impression he has formed of your company! So is the case at a job interview. Many candidates, though qualified, have sadly lost such wonderful opportunities, just because they were very poorly or shabbily presented. Because…90% of lasting impressions are created in the first 90 seconds

A person forms an impression of you, usually in less than ten seconds, based on a combination of some of these attributes:

- ✓ *Posture, Walk*
- ✓ *Body language*
- ✓ *Attire, Clothing*
- ✓ *Physical characteristics*
- ✓ *Smile, Facial features*
- ✓ *Handshake*
- ✓ *Cleanliness, Grooming*
- ✓ *Scent, perfume*
- ✓ *Eye contact*
- ✓ *Perceived Confidence*

In a study, men and women were asked to list the attributes they found attractive and unattractive in someone they met. And here is the list of some of the top responses:

Qualities that create a Positive Impression:

- ✓ Warmth
- ✓ Sense of humor
- ✓ Imagination
- ✓ Fitness
- ✓ Individuality
- ✓ Positive body language
- ✓ Conversational ability
- ✓ Kindness

Qualities that create a Negative Impression

- ✓ Self-centered
- ✓ Closed minded
- ✓ Judgmental
- ✓ Lack of manners
- ✓ Poor conversational ability
- ✓ Negative attitude
- ✓ Indecisiveness
- ✓ Lack of integrity
- ✓ Complaining and whining
- ✓ Politics and Power games
- ✓ Manipulation

Making a Great First Impression

If you want to make a good impression, know that you need to project **3 C's:**

- ✓ Confidence
- Have a straight but relaxed posture. Hold your head high and steady. Don't slouch or slump.
- Move in a natural, unaffected manner.
- Maintain eye contact with the people you are talking to.
- ✓ Competence
- Exhibit your knowledge when required. Know your way around the agenda. Be prepared for the meeting. Bring supportive materials to emphasize your points.
- Answer questions in a clear and professional manner, avoiding the use of slang or technical jargon.
- Ask relevant questions if needed.
- ✓ Credibility
- Arrive on time.
- Be presentable (well-groomed and mindful of dress codes)

- Keep true to your word.
- When uncertain, err on the side of what you presume is conservatism. And be observant; check if people are becoming uncomfortable.
- Etiquette mishaps can range from merely embarrassing to potentially insulting to the other person. When you realize that you have committed a faux pas, apologize immediately and ask how you can make up for it

Appearance IS Everything! It starts with your Personal Grooming

Paying attention to your grooming by taking care of your cleanliness and your clothing demonstrates respect for yourself and for others- the key words being neat and clean.

- ✓ A general rule of thumb is: the more expensive the products/services you sell, the more professional you should look-Customers make assumptions about you based on your appearance.
- ✓ If it's an expensive product you are selling, the customer is bound to think: "How can this person help us make this expensive purchase when he can't even afford a proper wardrobe and take care of himself?"

Projecting the Right Image!

- ✓ How you dress, how you groom yourself and how you handle yourself in public is all part of your "packaging"
- ✓ Like product packaging, you can present yourself to be most appealing. And, you can present yourself differently according to the time and place.

- ✓ Presence is how you “present” yourself- it’s your self-confidence, poise and appeal.

So what does it take to make a Special, Positive, and Instant Impression when prospective ‘buyers’ first see you.

According to Drew Westen, in his fabulous book "The Political Brain" one of the main determinants of electoral success," he explains, "is simply a candidate's curb appeal”. Curb appeal is the feeling voters get when they 'drive by' a candidate a few times on television and form an emotional impression! Personal Curb Appeal is primarily a nonverbal process.

How's your Personal Curb Appeal? When your co-workers, bosses, clients, and work partners "drive by" you, how do you come across? Here are a few tips to keep in mind:

- ✓ Dress for success: Always dress and see yourself for the next level!
- ✓ Your motto should be: "Wear great clothes. You never know whom you'll meet!" When it comes to curb appeal, the way you dress matters. Clothing has an effect on both the observer and the wearer.
- ✓ Dressing for success doesn't necessarily mean you have to wear a suit to work. Many organizations have a more casual dress code. But it does mean that whatever you wear should help you make the statement that you are a competent professional.

The finest clothing made is a person's skin, but, of course, society demands something more than this- Mark Twain

Watch your Body Language: People go by what they see!

As we've seen, people form 90% of their opinion of us in the first 90 seconds, a good example of just how powerful first impressions are! Being dressed for success is good but not enough in the competitive times in which we live. How many people do you know that impress us with their clothes but fail to impress us in other ways? Body language is the way you stand, sit, the way you move, and the way you present yourself. A major percentage of what we communicate has nothing to do with words, as we've seen in the earlier chapter.

We communicate in a lot of other ways-by the way we sit, stand, tense our facial muscles, tap our fingers, shuffle our feet and uncross or cross our legs. Without saying a word, our body language is broadcasting so many things about us!

So here are some quick tips on what to do and not do!

How to Look Interested

- ✓ Make strong eye contact
- ✓ Tilt your head slightly
- ✓ Don't fidget
- ✓ Look upward
- ✓ Lean forward slightly, weight on balls of feet.

When someone is friendly, we also think of him as trustworthy, sincere and reliable.

How to Stand the Right Way

- ✓ Stand squarely in front of the person to whom you are speaking.
- ✓ It might sound strange, but you expose your heart and body.

- ✓ Don't turn sideways.
- ✓ Meet their eyes in a friendly but steady gaze.
- ✓ Smile in a warm, relaxed way
- ✓ Don't hold a book or purse in front of you or cross your arms.
- ✓ Use open hand gestures.

Maintaining the Right Physical Distance

- ✓ If you watch a crowd, you will notice that people stand at different distances from each other.
- ✓ Less than 18 inches: intimate
- ✓ 18 inches- 2.5 feet: close friends in a social gathering. You can hold out your arm and you can stick your thumb in the other person's ear! Try it!
- ✓ 2.5-4 feet: most people in a casual setting
- ✓ 4-12 feet: strangers
- ✓ 12 feet: a group of strangers
- ✓ If you get too close, the other person will grow tense or withdraw

Making Eye Contact

- ✓ The eyes have it. Well, they truly do, and can project confidence when there are no words.
- ✓ To be a good listener, let your eyes convey: "I'm listening"

Here are some Signs that can indicate Nervousness. Try to work on controlling these:

- ✓ Eyes darting back and forth
- ✓ Tensing of the body
- ✓ Contraction of the body
- ✓ Shifting one's weight from side to side
- ✓ Rocking in chair
- ✓ Crossing and uncrossing the arms or legs
- ✓ Tapping hands, fingers, or feet

- ✓ Adjusting or fiddling with pens, cups, eyeglasses, jewelry, clothing, fingernails, hair, or hands wringing hands
- ✓ Clearing the throat
- ✓ Coughing nervously
- ✓ Smiling nervously
- ✓ Biting the lip
- ✓ Looking down
- ✓ Chewing nails or picking cuticles
- ✓ Putting hands in pockets

And here are some Signs that can indicate Boredom. Try and work on controlling these too:

- ✓ Moving your body frequently
- ✓ Letting your eyes wander
- ✓ Gazing into the distance
- ✓ Glancing often at your watch
- ✓ Yawning
- ✓ Tapping fingers or feet
- ✓ Fidgeting
- ✓ Picking your fingers or nails
- ✓ Avoiding eye contact

Sitting, Standing and Walking the Right Way

The Right Way to Sit- for a Lady: If you are in someone's office or at a big social event, never sit, till you are given permission to do so. The hostess/ host/ employer may have planned on a particular place she would like you to sit. If no one offers you, then only take the seat of your choice. Walk towards the chair with good posture. Turn and feel the chair with the back of your knees, just to make sure that no one has "accidentally" moved the chair away. Sit down, keeping your back straight and your head up, while keeping your knees together and you hands in your lap. Cross your legs at the ankle or hold your feet together. In any event, make sure your knees are together

The Right Way to Sit- for a Gentleman: Walk to the chair with good posture, and as you approach the chair, unbutton your jacket, if you are wearing one. Sit tall with your back against the chair and knees slightly apart and both feet on the floor, with your hands resting just above your knees. When you stand up, remember to re-button your jacket

Standing: When you get up, keep your feet parallel but your knees relaxed. Ensure that your spine is long and straight, with your shoulders back, stomach in, chest high, chin turned up slightly and your arms and hands relaxed.

Walking: Stand as mentioned above and step with feet slightly ahead of your body. This promotes good posture

Other Points: Never lean on anything, as it denotes a careless attitude with 99% of your "presence" being lost when you lean.

Never greet someone with a handshake across the table (the only exception of course is when you're meeting someone and both of you are seated).

Always stand up when you are shaking hands. Greeting someone from behind a desk creates an instant barrier. Instead, always greet someone as your equal

Assessing Your Skills

Assessing and showcasing your skills effectively is a pivotal aspect of succeeding in job interviews. This chapter will delve into understanding the skills employers desire, providing examples of how to demonstrate these skills, comprehending interview structures and stages, preparing for technical interviews, mastering case studies, and navigating commonly asked interview questions with suggested answers.

Desired Skills

Before entering an interview, it's crucial to identify and understand the skills that employers value in potential candidates. Desired skills often vary based on the industry, role, and company culture.

Example: For a marketing role, employers may seek candidates with strong communication skills, creativity, data analysis proficiency, and the ability to adapt to rapidly changing trends.

Action Plan:

- ✓ Review Job Descriptions: Analyze job descriptions for roles you are interested in to identify commonly sought-after skills.
- ✓ Self-Assessment: Reflect on your own experiences and identify instances where you have demonstrated these skills.
- ✓ Skill Development: Work on enhancing or acquiring skills through coursework, workshops, or practical experiences.

Examples of Skills Used

Practical Application:

Understanding how to showcase your skills through concrete examples is key to making a lasting impression during an interview. Sharing specific instances where you successfully utilized a particular skill helps illustrate your capabilities.

Example: If teamwork is a desired skill, recount an experience where you collaborated with a diverse team to overcome a challenge, highlighting your role and the positive outcome.

Template: *"In my previous role at [Company], I was part of a cross-functional team tasked with [specific project]. I played a pivotal role in [describe your contributions], fostering effective communication and collaboration, which ultimately resulted in [positive outcome]."*

Action Plan:

- ✓ Identify Key Skills: List the skills required for the position and select those most relevant to your experiences.
- ✓ Create STAR Stories: Develop Situation, Task, Action, Result (STAR) stories for each skill to articulate your experiences effectively.
- ✓ Quantify Achievements: Where possible, quantify the impact of your contributions to demonstrate tangible results.

Example of Creating STAR Stories

An example of creating STAR stories for two skills relevant to a marketing role: "Project Management" and "Data Analysis." Each STAR story will include the Situation, Task, Action, and Result components.

Skill: Project Management

STAR Story: Organizing a Successful Product Launch Event

- ✓ Situation: During my role as a Marketing Coordinator at XYZ Company, we were launching a new product, and the company decided to host a product launch event to create buzz and engage key stakeholders.

- ✓ Task: I was tasked with coordinating the entire event, from planning logistics to ensuring effective communication among team members, vendors, and attendees. The goal was to create a seamless and memorable experience for our audience.
- ✓ Action:

  Detailed Planning: I initiated a detailed project plan outlining all the tasks, deadlines, and responsibilities.

  Collaborative Approach: I collaborated with cross-functional teams, including design, sales, and external vendors, to ensure everyone was aligned with the event objectives.

  Problem-Solving: When unexpected challenges arose, such as last-minute changes in venue availability, I quickly identified alternative solutions and communicated changes effectively to the team.
- ✓ Result: The product launch event was a tremendous success. Attendees praised the seamless organization, engaging presentations, and overall atmosphere. The event led to a 30% increase in product awareness, generating positive media coverage and increased sales inquiries.

Skill: Data Analysis

STAR Story: Analyzing Marketing Campaign Effectiveness

- ✓ Situation: In my previous role as a Marketing Analyst at ABC Corporation, the company had invested significantly in digital marketing campaigns, and there was a need to assess the effectiveness of these campaigns to inform future strategies.

- ✓ Task: I was assigned the task of conducting a comprehensive analysis of the recent digital marketing campaigns, identifying key performance indicators, and providing actionable insights for optimization.
- ✓ Action:

  Data Collection: I collected data from various sources, including Google Analytics, social media platforms, and email marketing tools.

  Metrics Identification: I identified relevant metrics such as click-through rates, conversion rates, and engagement metrics to measure campaign performance.

  Data Visualization: Using tools like Tableau, I created visually compelling reports and dashboards to communicate complex data trends and insights effectively.
- ✓ Result: The analysis revealed areas of improvement in targeting and messaging, leading to strategic adjustments in subsequent campaigns. By implementing the recommended changes, we observed a 20% increase in conversion rates and a 15% decrease in cost per acquisition, contributing to a more efficient and effective digital marketing strategy.

Interview Application:

During an interview, you can use these STAR stories to effectively articulate your experiences:

- ✓ Situation and Task: Clearly set the context by describing the situation and task, providing necessary background information.
- ✓ Action: Discuss your specific actions in a structured manner, emphasizing your skills and contributions.
- ✓ Result: Highlight the positive outcomes and measurable results of your actions. Quantifiable achievements add credibility to your story.

Remember to tailor your STAR stories to the specific skills and experiences relevant to the job you're interviewing for. This approach helps interviewers understand not only what you've done but also how your actions led to positive outcomes in various situations.

Self-Assessment: Personal and Professional Skills Evaluation

Below is a detailed template for assessing one's skills, traits, attributes, attitude & behavior, and competency skills. The evaluation is based on a scale of 1 to 5, where 1 represents the lowest proficiency and 5 indicates the highest proficiency. This template can serve as a self-assessment tool for candidates to identify their strengths and areas for improvement.

I. Personal Attributes and Traits:

Adaptability:
(1) Struggles to adapt to new situations.
(5) Quickly adapts to changes, thriving in dynamic environments.

Resilience:
(1) Easily overwhelmed by setbacks.
(5) Demonstrates resilience in the face of challenges, bouncing back quickly.

Time Management:
(1) Poor at prioritizing and often misses deadlines.
(5) Exceptional time management, consistently meets or exceeds deadlines.

Initiative:
(1) Waits for direction before taking action.
(5) Proactively identifies and tackles tasks without constant guidance.

Communication Skills:
(1) Struggles to convey thoughts and ideas clearly.
(5) Communicates articulately and effectively in various situations.

II. Attitude and Behavior:

Teamwork:

(1) Has difficulty collaborating with others.

(5) Excels in team environments, fostering collaboration.

Leadership:

(1) Reluctant to take on leadership roles.

(5) Inspires and guides others effectively, demonstrating leadership qualities.

Professionalism:

(1) Displays unprofessional behavior.

(5) Consistently maintains a high level of professionalism in all interactions.

Adaptability:

(1) Resistant to change.

(5) Embraces change positively and adapts seamlessly.

III. Competency Skills:

Problem-Solving:

(1) Struggles to find effective solutions to challenges.

(5) Analyzes problems adeptly, providing innovative solutions.

Technical Proficiency:

(1) Lacks proficiency in required technical skills.

(5) Highly skilled in relevant technical areas, continuously updates knowledge.

Decision-Making:

(1) Makes poor decisions without careful consideration.

(5) Makes well-informed decisions, weighing all factors.

Overall Self-Assessment:

1-10 Points: Significant improvement needed.
11-20 Points: Below average; focus on development areas.
21-30 Points: Average proficiency; consider improvement opportunities.
31-40 Points: Above average; continue refining skills.
41-50 Points: Exceptional proficiency; leverage strengths for career advancement.

Action Plan for Improvement:

- ✓ Identify the top three areas for improvement based on your self-assessment.
- ✓ Set specific, measurable goals for each improvement area.
- ✓ Create a timeline for achieving these goals.
- ✓ Seek resources, training, or mentorship to support your development.
- ✓ Regularly reassess your progress and adjust your action plan accordingly.

This comprehensive self-assessment template enables you to evaluate your skills systematically, providing a clear roadmap for improvement. Regularly revisiting this assessment can aid in tracking progress and fostering continuous personal and professional development.

Preparing a WINNING Resume

Resume Preparing

Let's first understand what is a Resume and its Importance?

A resume is a document that you, the jobseeker-uses to promote your skills, abilities, and knowledge to a potential employer-It is the gateway to landing an interview for a job or just an internship. It should display your experience, skills, education and accomplishments. Résumés vary in length, but are typically one page for undergraduates and two pages for graduate students with professional experience. It uses your past experiences and accomplishments to position you for a current or for future opportunities. From an employer's perspective, resumes are used to identify qualified candidates to invite to an interview. The primary purpose of your resume is to get the reader's attention and make that person want to know more, that is, to get an interview. It is not a comprehensive history of your entire work life. Rather, it is a sales sheet, and you are the product. On average, employers spend only 5-7 seconds reviewing your résumé the first time they see it, so layout, presentation and format are key!

A poorly written resume may very well prevent you from getting that interview; and without an interview, you won't get the job, as resumes do not generate job offers, but well written resumes do facilitate interviews. They are only a marketing tool. The resume is important, but just one of several steps that make up a successful job search.

To the Employer reading your resume, it must address these questions. So think carefully before you start on preparing your resume:

- ✓ Who you are?
- ✓ The position you are applying for?
- ✓ The skills and qualifications you have?
- ✓ The work experience you have that directly relates to the job you're applying for?
- ✓ Will you be the right fit for the position?
- ✓ Will you be able to solve challenges and problems and the value you will bring to the employer if you get hired?
- ✓ What is it that you will bring to the organization that they may not get with other candidates? What differentiates you from others?
- ✓ How will hiring you benefit them in the long term?

Key Points to keep in mind before you start on your resume:

- ✓ **The Most Important Key: Customize your skills on every resume you send out to match the job offer requirements.**
- ✓ When you pick up your résumé, notice where are your thumbs? They are probably at about the midpoint of the page. This is where most employers spend 15 – 30 seconds when first examining a résumé- only seeing the top half of your résumé. Therefore, everything above your thumb should be the most important information that you want to convey to the employer, and everything below your thumb should support the message you are communicating. Research reveals that if you haven't presented the most important information about yourself in the top half of the

first page of your resume, you can probably forget about getting the job. If in that brief time, the prospective employer does not see anything that gets their attention, then they reject the resume. Employers want to quickly screen out applicants, but your goal must be to get screened in.

- ✓ Put strong statements at the beginning of your résumé. The most important information should come first.
- ✓ Your Resume is your very first contact in most cases. Remember- First Impressions matter and there are only 3 entrances to any business: The front door, the telephone and the internet/post (most resumes are that first contact) to create this first impression ...and if either of these are not impressive, you have lost your opportunity forever! So make sure that it gives a positive, professional impression.
- ✓ Avoid Templates: Do not use one of the Resume Wizards or Templates that are available online. They can be difficult to work with, and don't allow you to present yourself in a way that makes you unique. Employers can identify them easily! Instead, create your resume as a simple document in MS Word
- ✓ Objective: Why are you sending the résumé? Will it achieve the purpose? You must know your objective.
- ✓ Focus on achievements: What separates you from everyone else? What are your differentiators? Why should they hire you?
- ✓ Accuracy: Check dates/ information? Dig! Find out!

- ✓ Clarity and Simplicity: This is not the time to try to use big tongue-twisting words in your document.
- ✓ Presentation and layout: Must get one's attention right away. It must sell! What measurable facts can you provide? It must have a feeling and sense of a person behind the resume-This flat piece of paper must be so vibrant and impressive that the employer will want to meet you in person. It must address 'what's in it for them'
- ✓ Credibility: More than 80% of résumés contain some stretch of the truth. Don't do this. Don't lie or embellish the truth (employers will check your references) And if you lose your professionalism, it will be nearly impossible to get it back
- ✓ Vague Claims vs Accomplishments:
  "Excellent written communication skills"
  "Wrote jargon-free User Guide for XXXX users"
  "Team player with cross-functional skills"
  "Collaborated with clients, Accounts Receivables and Sales to increase speed of receivables and prevent interruption of service to clients."
  "Demonstrated success in analyzing client needs"
  "Created and implemented comprehensive needs assessment mechanisms to help forecast demand for services and staffing."
- ✓ Remember the 3-Example Rule: If you list a skill, you need to be ready to come up with three examples to support it. Keep them ready with you

✓ Key Words: These days, applicant tracking systems scan resumes for keywords that match the company's job descriptions. So use words in your resume that match the job description. Highlight how you meet the competencies detailed in the posting, using keywords or skills listed in the job posting. If the keywords/skills are missing, your resume may be rejected.

✓ Use action/ power words: When describing what you have done-use 'Power Words' (See samples)

Power Verbs

Avoid using generic terms when describing your skills and experiences. Instead, use this list to find the right words to appropriately explain why you are the ideal candidate for the job for which you are applying.

accomplished
achieved
acted
adapted
administered
advertised
advised
analyzed
applied
approved
arranged
assigned
assisted
attained
attended
audited
authorized
budgeted
calculated
clarified
coached
collected
communicated
completed
compiled
composed
conducted
consolidated
consulted
contributed
controlled
coordinated
corrected
created
defined
delegated
demonstrated
designed
determined
developed
devised
diagnosed
directed
distributed
documented
drafted
edited
enforced
engineered
established
estimated
evaluated
examined
exhibited
expanded
experimented
explained
expressed
facilitated
filed
formulated
furnished
gathered
generated
guided
handled
hired
identified
illustrated
implemented
improved
increased
informed
influenced
initiated
inspected
installed
instructed
integrated
interpreted
interviewed
introduced
invented
investigated
led
listened
managed
manufactured
marketed
measured
mediated
monitored
negotiated
obtained
operated
ordered
organized
originated
participated
performed
persuaded
photographed
pioneered
planned
predicted
prepared
presented
presided
printed
processed
produced
programmed
promoted
proposed
provided
publicized
published
purchased
recommended
reconciled
recorded
recruited
referred
repaired
reported
represented
researched
resolved
responded
retrieved
reviewed
revised
scheduled
selected
sold
served
simplified
solved
strengthened
studied
submitted
summarized
supervised
supplied
surveyed
tabulated
taught
tested
trained
transcribed
transformed
translated
tutored
verified
wrote

- ✓ Fonts: Keep typeface/fonts simple-one that is universal; and will open on any system. It's best to use Times-Roman or Arial. Use 11 or 12-point type. Do not use graphics unless you are in the design field.
- ✓ Your name should be big and bold at the top of the page.
- ✓ Use all caps, bold, or italics for important headings and titles, but don't overdo it
- ✓ Balance white space with text space so the resume doesn't look crowded in some sections and empty in others
- ✓ Resumes for recent college graduates should be one page. Other experienced professionals with enough relevant experience to fill the second page, may want to create two page resumes.
- ✓ Justify the left margin, but not the right. It's easier to read.
- ✓ The word "I" is used only in the cover letter
- ✓ Proof-read, Proof-read, and again Proof-read: One mistake generally means you are out of the door. The quality of your résumé reflects the quality of your work and professionalism. If you make a mistake on your résumé, will you make a mistake in your job? Employers will think so.
- ✓ Print out: Print on 8 1/2" x 11" white or light colored, good quality paper. Avoid flashy colors. Use conservative colors like white, off-white, beige or gray parchment. Use matching paper for cover letter and avoid folding your résumé into a mailing envelope. Send it in a 9" x 11" mailing envelope.

Resume Formats

There is no "best" or "right" way to prepare your resume. The key is to use a format that will present you and your qualifications in the best possible light- and make the interviewer want to know more. Given below are two most common resume formats along with some general guidelines to help you decide which is best for you.

1. The Chronological Format

This is the most common resume format, and the one most familiar to employers. With this format, you present your work history in chronological order, starting with your present or most recent job and working backward. Job titles, employers and dates of employment are emphasized, with duties and accomplishments and results listed under each job.

Chronological Resume Format

Your Full Name
Street Address,
City, State, Pin code
Phone Number / Cell Number
E-mail Address

Objective: A one or two sentence summary of your accomplishments and your career objective. This should be specifically targeted to the job you're applying for.

Work Experience

20XX- Present **Your Job Title** **Employer, Employer's City, State**

A one sentence description of your responsibilities.

- Using three to five bullet points, include short, concisely written accomplishments, listed individually. Use specific facts and figures to support your statements.
- List a second accomplishment.
- List a third accomplishment.
- List a fourth accomplishment. Since this is your most recent job, include more information about it. For subsequent jobs, list fewer points. Be sure to list specific skills you used to succeed.

20## - 20## **Your Job Title** **Employer, Employer's City, State**

A one sentence description of your responsibilities.

- Using two to four bullet points, include short, concisely written accomplishments, listed individually. Use specific facts and figures to support your statements.
- List a second accomplishment.

Education

School Name (City, State)
Major, Percentage, Highest Degree Earned, Graduation Date

Advantages: It emphasizes continuity and career progression in employment, highlights job titles and names of employers, easy to follow, and most familiar to employers.

Best used: When your career direction is clear and your career objective is consistent with your education and work history, when the name of a job title or employer adds prestige to your resume, when your work history shows steady job progression and/or advancement.

2. The Functional Format

Functional Resume Format

Your Full Name
Street Address,
City, State,
Pin code
Phone,
E-mail

Objective / Job Title You're Pursuing
In one or two sentences, explain your specific career goal(s) or convey to the reader what job title you're looking to fill and why you're qualified.

Experience
List Your Most Marketable Skill (It must relate directly to the job you're pursuing)

- List your most impressive achievement using that skill, followed by the name of the employer and the employer's city and state.
- List a second achievement you've accomplished using that skill thus far in your professional career and the employer information.
- List a third achievement and the employer information. Since this is your most marketable skill—the biggest reason why you should be hired, use up to five bullet points.

List Your Second Most Marketable Skill

- Include up to three bullets describing how you've used this skill thus far in your career. Each bullet should include one example and list the name of the employer, plus the employer's city and state.
- List another example of how you've used this skill successfully.

List Your Third Most Marketable Skill

- Include up to three bullets describing how you've used this skill thus far in your career. Each bullet should include one example and list the name of the employer, plus the employer's city and state.
- List another example of how you've used this skill successfully.

Provide Another Reason Why You're Qualified For The Job You're Applying For

- List up to three or four achievements, areas of proficiency, specific skills, etc. (using separate bullets) that the employer will find impressive.

Employment History

20ZZ - Present	**Job Title**	**Employer's Name, Employer's City, State**
20## - 20xx	**Job Title**	**Employer's Name, Employer's City, State**
(List each employer)		

Education
Include a listing of degrees earned, the educational institution(s), graduation dates, etc.

This format allows you to highlight and emphasize your skills and highest competencies. Here, you list major skill areas and describe accomplishments that illustrates your proficiency in each skill area. These accomplishments are usually derived from a variety of work experiences and are arranged under each major skill area rather than under the position you held at the time. Using this format, the Work History section of your resume contains only the job titles, employers and dates of employment.

Advantages: It emphasizes skills and competencies, allows considerable flexibility in describing your professional experiences, de-emphasizes work history, and eliminates repetition in listing jobs where the duties are the same or very similar.

Best used: When you are making a career change or have little or no work experience that is relevant to your career objective, when you have significant gaps in your employment history or are reentering the job market after a long absence, when you have held the same job or been doing the same type of work for an extended time, when you want to emphasize a particularly strong set of skills or strengths.

Resume Headings & Sections

1. Identification/ Heading: Every resume must begin with personal contact information. The heading should include your name, current mailing address, phone number and email. Be sure to list a phone number that will reach you as an employer may call or message you at any time. If you are listing your cell phone, label it as a cell or mobile number and record an appropriate voicemail greeting. There are

no strict rules about how the heading must look, but given below in the illustration are a few examples

Identification Heading Samples

Jonathan Peters

Jonathan.Peters@hotmail.com • +91 94440-36524 (Cell)
19/18, Central Street • Colaba • Mumbai-400005

Jonathan Peters

Jonathan.Peters@hotmail.com • +91 94440-36524 (Cell) •19/18, Central Street • Colaba • Mumbai-400005

Jonathan Peters Jonathan.Peters@hotmail.com • +91 94440-36524 (Cell)
19/18, Central Street • Colaba • Mumbai-400005

Career Objective or Profile Summary

A **Senior Human Resources Professional** with over 12 years of in-depth knowledge & progressive experience in benefits management, including defined contribution, health and welfare, stock purchase, and pension plans; conflict resolution, and arbitration with national-level corporations now seeks a Senior Level Position in a Multi-National setup

A highly experienced **Sales and Marketing Professional** with extensive strategic planning and implementation skills and over $39 million in total profit improvement added in 7 years; seeks a position as a Sales Manager where these skills will help add similar or greater value.

2. Career Objective/ Profile Summary: By having an objective it will help you develop a clear focused and targeted resume and can help in determining what to include in the rest of your resume. Ensure that the objective includes the position or at least the career field for which you are applying. The objective must be short and specific, with your areas of greatest expertise, your principal skills, and a statement of your career ambition that you have to offer the employer, not what you want the employer to do for you. It can sometimes include your professional goals and explain how you plan to achieve them in the role for which you're applying and must be ideally

not more than three to four sentences long. This section delivers an impact at the top of your resume - it's the first impression. The statements should match your skills to the target job description. You want the employers to read the summary and say "we have to meet this person." Information in this section must be customized to fit each position you apply for. Place most important words first since the scanner may be limited in the number of words it reads. This will help the potential employer to look at your resume in a more positive light, given the few seconds that they take to glance at each resume. See examples.

3. Qualifications/ Education and Training: Here, you want to list the schools/colleges attended with dates, degrees and any honors you received. You should also include any relevant training classes, seminars or workshops you may have completed in addition to your formal education.

Educational Qualifications

Loyalty College, (Pondicherry University) Mumbai, INDIA
Masters in Business Administration in Sales & Marketing; 2007 to 2009

Loyalty College, (Madras University) Chennai, INDIA
Bachelor of Arts in Economics; 2004 to 2007

Professional Experience

Global Key Account Manager Sept 2018- Present
Tomashika Worldwide Inc , Mumbai, INDIA

- Oversaw direct sales efforts for the company's largest commercial account, positioning the client as a strategic business partner
- Participated in account development for key sales and contract negotiations and prepared sales forecasts and status reports, making recommendations to management to enhance revenue growth
- Planned, developed, and participated in formulation and implementation of strategy, primarily for XXXX and ZZZZ services, as well as the global portfolio of GGGGGG and HHHHH in Europe, Asia Pacific, and South America
- Grew revenue from $22 million to over $75 million annually by targeting new business opportunities and demonstrating competitively priced, quality service
- As additional Responsibilities, handled the SE Asian (VVVV Division)

4. Professional Experience/Work History: This section should include those work experiences (both paid and unpaid) that relate to the position you are seeking. What do you want the organization to learn about you from reviewing your experiences? It must highlight your most relevant experiences and can include volunteer, leadership, work, internship, and/or extracurricular experiences. Always keep in mind the answer to the question “how can you contribute to our company?” when working on this section. To draw the organization’s attention use more than one experience section with titles that emphasize the specific types of experiences that connect with the employer. Include title, name of organization, location (city/state) and dates (month/year). Describe experiences highlighting skills used/gained and tangible accomplishments.

Here are some tips to help you describe your experiences

Begin by making a list: Brainstorm for a few minutes about each of your experiences. Think beyond just jobs and internships to volunteer and leadership experiences. Write down any and all contributions that come to mind, even if they seem insignificant. Ask yourself:

- ✓ What did I do above and beyond my normal duties? How did I take initiative?
- ✓ What transferable skills did I use?
- ✓ How did I stand out among other employees, such as consistently meeting or exceeding goals, deadlines or quotas?
- ✓ Was I ever praised or recognized for a job well done? Did I receive any positive feedback, accolades, awards, or promotions?

- ✓ Did I develop and/or implement any new processes or make suggestions that improved things?
- ✓ What problems did I solve?
- ✓ Did I save the company money or time?
- ✓ What made me really great at my job?
- ✓ What am I most proud of?
- ✓ What are my strongest skills?

Next craft into bulleted statements:

- ✓ Use action verbs and phrases (rather than full sentences) to keep the language action oriented and focused on skills and accomplishments- using the appropriate tense
- ✓ Mention the scope of your activities (e.g., number of staff managed, size of event, percentage of increase/decrease, number of articles written weekly). When they are in your favor, quantify with numbers
- ✓ Detail the results (the added value), which could be the outcome of your actions for the company or customers or specific skills you gained or demonstrated in that experience. Focus on the skill sets that might be relevant to the position
- ✓ Take care to tailor your selections to the job you are applying for. List them in order of importance/ relevance for each application.
- ✓ Use the “bullet plus” concept shown in the illustration to strengthen your descriptions. Include what you did plus how, why or the impact of your work. (See sample)

Write a "Bullet Plus"

Use the **"bullet plus"** concept to strengthen your descriptions. Include what you did plus how, why or the impact of your work.

When writing a bullet plus use the formula:
Action Verb + What + How/Why/Impact

Example: Interpersonal & Relationship skills (This is the 'What')
Developed Interpersonal & Relationship skills ('Developed 'is the Action Word+ What)
Bullet plus: Developed Interpersonal & Relationship Skills by facilitating cross-cultural conversations with Asian & Arabic Businessmen and Chamber of Commerce Members. (How)

It is not necessary to list every job you have ever held, but be sure to list those that demonstrate how you have developed and effectively used your skills and abilities in the work setting. You also want to show a steady work history with no lengthy gaps in employment, if possible. Thus, it may be important to include jobs you held while going to school, even if they aren't directly relevant to your career objective.

When listing your experience, maintain reverse chronological order, starting with your most recent position and working backwards. If you have meaningful relevant experience in the past, but now have a job in an unrelated field, you might divide this section into two separate sections: "Relevant Experience" and "Other Experience." This will allow you to put your most relevant experience closer to the top of your resume (under "Relevant Experience") and the less relevant information next on the page, (under "Other Experience").

5. Other Activities (Other possible titles: Leadership Roles/ Volunteering Experience/ Professional Affiliations): Under this section, which usually follows work experience, you might want to list and describe your additional activities. This can be especially helpful for recent graduates who may have only limited or no work experience thus far. The title of this section will vary, depending on the type of activities you choose to list. Be sure to select those which are the most recent, relevant, and professional –those that best demonstrate your skills and abilities. Always make sure to include the name of the organization, the location (city and state), your title or position if applicable, dates of affiliation and the activities carried out/ undertaken, describing responsibilities of the position and your accomplishments within the organization. Always start from the most recent ones.

Other Activities

- Emerging HR Professionals, Editorial Board , Mumbai, India: (Sept 2016 – Present)
- All India Management Club, Mumbai , Training Coordinator (2020- Present)
- Future Business Leaders of INDIA, Secretary (2021-22),
- Throne Room Worship Church, Sunday Worship Leader, Mumbai, (2018-2021)
  Also assisted with craft projects, music lessons and addressed behavioral issues of teens
- St Johns Hospital, Cuffe Parade, Mumbai (2012-2014)
  Visited patients & family members, providing social and emotional support

Skills

Computer: HRIS; PeopleSoft;
Microsoft Word, Excel and PowerPoint
Languages: Proficient in French (written/ spoken)
Arabic (spoken)
Other: Professional in Human Resources (PHR) Certification
Proof Reading Skills
Content Writing

Professional Recognition

CEO's Achievement Award, 2022
Centre of Excellence Award, 2021
Selected as Ambassador from 1,000 candidates for the Emerging Leaders Program, 2015
Young HR Leader Award, 2012

Associations

Member, All India Human Resources & Labor Management Association 2018-Present
Member, Asian Marketing Association 2017-Present

6. Skills: This is the place where you may list other specific skills that are relevant to the position you are applying for. If you have any special certifications or trainings that you know can help, you might wish to include that information here too. Some examples could be proof reading skills, content writing, any other languages etc

7. Other Possible Headings: Depending on your particular strengths and experiences, there are various other headings which can be used. Some suggestions: Professional Organizations and Associations, Professional Recognition/ Honors and Awards, Community Service and Volunteer Activities, Special Skills or Technical Specialties

8. References: As a general rule, you should never list names of references on your resume. If necessary- to round out the visual representation of your resume, you may include the phrase "References furnished upon request" as a final statement in the same style as your other major headings. But it is also most acceptable to omit this statement altogether. Create a separate reference page and bring it with you to the interview. Include the reference names, titles, organization/company names, business addresses, phone numbers, and email addresses of each reference. Include only those persons who have agreed to serve as a reference for you. List all your personal information at the top of this page. (See sample)

Obtaining References: Speak directly with the people you are planning to name as references (prior employers, faculty members, etc.). Let them know the kinds of jobs you are applying for and what specific kinds of experiences and abilities you hope they can discuss about you. Give them a copy of your resume to refer to when called.

Sample Reference Page

Jonathan Peters
123 Central Street,
Colaba,
Mumbai

References

Dr. John Roberts
Professor of Psychology
University of Mumbai
Mumbai
Tel: (022) 26847589

Mr. Philip Joshua
President & CEO
Hessed Consulting Ltd,
Cuffe Parade,
Mumbai
Tel: +91 XXXXX YYYY ZZ

Ms. Susan Jeremiah
Attorney
Mumbai High Court
Mumbai
Tel: (044) 28674538

Note: *Before you begin to lay out your resume, you may like to gather all your relevant information first under various headings. To help you do so, a blank 'Resume Worksheet Template' is provided to help you collate all such information. After you have gathered all, and after checking for the accuracy, you can then format it professionally in the way that best suits the job you are applying for using the suggestions provided above.*

Résumé Worksheet Template

Name
Address
Phone
E-mail

Job Objective

Highlights of Qualifications/ Summary of Experience
Skill Clusters (Use relevant titles such as Sales/ Selling Skills, Customer Service, Computer Skills, Management Skills, etc.)
•Skill 1

•Skill 2

•Skill 3

•Skill 4

Work History
Employer
Location
Dates: To Position or Title
List as many responsibilities, accomplishments or results that describe your performance

Employer
Location
Dates: To Position or Title
List as many responsibilities, accomplishments or results that describe your performance

Employer
Location
Dates: To Position or Title
List as many responsibilities, accomplishments or results that describe your performance

Education
University
City, State
Diploma, Degree, Certificate or Field of Study
Date (only if very recent

University
City, State
Diploma, Degree, Certificate or Field of Study
Date (only if very recent

Additional Training/ Education
Community or Volunteer Work
Additional Information

Résumé Final Checklist **Yes/ No**

1. Material fits neatly on one page, two pages if there is enough relevant experience.
2. No spelling, grammar or punctuation errors.
3. Typing is neat, clean and professional-looking.
4. Name, address, telephone and e-mail are at the top and easy to locate.
5. Margins at sides and bottom are not less than one-half inch.
6. Layout and design are easy to read and pleasing to the eye.
7. Important titles are emphasized by using text enhancements where appropriate (caps, bolds, underline, italics), but not overdone.
8. Indentations or appropriate symbols are used to organize information logically.
9. Overall appearance invites one to read it.
10. Action words are used to communicate accomplishments and results.
11. Extraneous personal information (height, weight, age, sex, etc.) has been omitted.
12. If using a career objective, make sure it is specific, clear and targeted.
13. Remember the RULE OF THUMB - the most important information is in the first half.
14. Use conservative colors like white, off-white, beige or gray parchment.
15. Avoid graphics and colorful paper unless you are in the design field.
16. Always use reverse chronological order.
17. Employment that is older than 15 years may not be listed.
18. Language specific only to the company in which you worked has been translated to apply to other areas (spell out acronyms).
19. Strongest statements are at the top, working downward from them.
20. Dates of employment and education are included and accurate.
21. "References Available Upon Request" has been replaced with more skills. References are listed on a separate sheet of paper.
22. Quantities, amounts and dollar values are used to enhance the description your job.
23. Addresses and phone numbers of previous employers are omitted.
24. Hobbies or social skills are not listed unless they are related to the job target.
25. The word "I" is used only in the cover letter.
26. If I am changing careers, my transferable skills are easily identifiable.
27. I feel that my résumé represents me well.

The Cover Letter: Your Personal Brand

A cover letter is a very important piece of your "personal brand" plan that describes your unique skills and strengths that can make you attractive and stand out from the rest to an employer. The cover letter needs to be crafted to entice the potential employer to read your résumé further, convey your enthusiasm and motivation, highlighting specific interest in the position and organization, by emphasizing on your specific skills and achievements, and providing the reader with a professional example of your writing ability. The purpose of a cover letter is to ignite an employer's interest in you as a candidate. So this is your opportunity to elaborate on your expertise and experience and show the employer that you are the best match for the opportunity. Each cover letter must be tailored to the organization and position. No two cover letters should look the same! Analyze the description of the position carefully, pick out key phrases and infuse them into your document. Match your letter to the requirements point by point by emphasizing key parts of your résumé.

Few key points on how it needs to be:

- ✓ It needs to be specifically worded and targeted for the position you are applying for.
- ✓ The letter should never be a standard, generic one
- ✓ It must be checked for spelling and grammar, as this is the first impression- and can be the last. Many recruiters will dismiss even the most qualified candidate if there is only one

typo or grammar error. Reread your letter two or three times, and then ask yet another person to review it.

- ✓ Keep it short-Tell your story. The ideal cover letter must be roughly a 3/4-page to a full page in length. A concise letter demonstrates that you are focused and have strong communication skills.
- ✓ State the position and source in the first paragraph of the letter, as chances are that the recruiter who reads your letter may be hiring for several positions. So clearly state the job title preferably in the first sentence, and how you learned of the position
- ✓ Do your groundwork and make it clear in your cover letter that you have researched the organization and understand their mission and overall work.
- ✓ Focus on your key strengths, not on your weaknesses. Your job is to convince the recruiter you are qualified, so keep the letter positive.
- ✓ Clearly mention ways of how you intend to contribute, (not what you expect to benefit), by maybe even providing one or two specific examples of how your skills, experiences and qualities directly fit the company's needs and position description.
- ✓ Avoid beating around the bush with phrases such as: "I am writing to…" or "Let me introduce myself."
- ✓ Avoid too many I's
- ✓ The cover letter would need to demonstrate to the employer that you are the solution to their employment issue. Clearly state how the

position fits into your overall career plans and what you find exciting about the opportunity and the organization. Aim to grab the attention of the reader in the first paragraph

Sample Cover Letter

Jonathan Peters
123 Central Street,
Colaba,
Mumbai

[Date]

Mr. Philip Joshua
President & CEO
Hessed Engineering Consulting Ltd.
Cuffe Parade,
Mumbai

Dear Mr. Joshua:

As a recent graduate in industrial engineering, I am interested in joining Hessed Engineering Consulting Ltd. My interest in your organization was sparked during a series of projects I completed as part of my engineering training. I believe you are in need of talented people, so let me tell you why you should consider me for an interview.

Pursuit of excellence: I graduated in the top 3 percent of my engineering class., and was always consistent in my performance.

Project experience: Through class assignments and part-time jobs, I demonstrated the ability to be a productive member of technical project teams.

Understanding your methods: The same production process you utilize for clients was highlighted in two projects and one research paper that I completed for my degree.

For more detailed information on my experience and skills, please see my enclosed resume.

I would deeply appreciate the opportunity to visit Hessed Engineering Consulting Ltd; an organization I have admired a lot for a few years now.

I look forward to hearing from you to schedule a time to meet.

Thank you for your consideration.
Sincerely,

Jonathan Peters

Enclosure

This would ideally be the flow for a cover letter:
First paragraph: Attract the employer's interest by briefly touching on your specific interest in the company and/or position and showing you have researched the company. If you have been referred by someone or met a recruiter at a career event, here is where you mention it. You want to convince them by clearly explaining why you want to work for

them and how you would contribute to the organization- why you are a strong candidate.

Middle paragraph: Select a few examples of your experiences, skills, and qualities that match the position and show how you are uniquely qualified. This is the place to “tell your story” and show what you bring to the table. You can refer to key aspects of the résumé which relate to the job or employer, but do not simply list items from your résumé. A cover letter should build on the résumé, not restate it!

Closing paragraph: Reiterate your interest and enthusiasm for the position. Request an interview and indicate how and when you can be contacted. Maybe even suggest that you will call to discuss interview possibilities. Thank the reader for their time and consideration.

Understanding the Interview Structure and Stages

Being familiar with the structure and stages of an interview helps candidates navigate the process more effectively. Interviews commonly consist of an introduction, skill assessment, and closing stages.
Example: A structured interview may include an initial icebreaker, skill-based questions, a task or assessment, and a segment for questions from the candidate.

Action Plan:

- ✓ Research Company Practices: Investigate the interview format commonly used by the company, either through online resources or by networking with current or former employees.
- ✓ Prepare for Each Stage: Anticipate the different stages of the interview and tailor your preparation accordingly.
- ✓ Understand Timing: Be mindful of time constraints and ensure your responses are concise and focused.

Handling Technical Interviews

Strategies: Technical interviews assess a candidate's proficiency in specific skills relevant to the job. Preparation involves reviewing technical concepts, practicing problem-solving, and demonstrating a systematic approach.
Example: For a software engineering position, a technical interview might involve coding exercises,

algorithmic problem-solving, and discussions about system architecture.

Action Plan:

- ✓ Review Job Requirements: Identify the technical skills mentioned in the job description.
- ✓ Practice Coding: Engage in coding practice sessions on platforms like LeetCode or HackerRank.
- ✓ Seek Feedback: Collaborate with peers or mentors for mock technical interviews to receive constructive feedback.

Preparing for Case Studies

Approach: Case studies assess a candidate's ability to analyze and solve real-world problems. Effectively preparing involves understanding the industry, practicing structured problem-solving, and presenting solutions clearly.

Example: For a consulting role, a case study might involve analyzing a client's business challenge and proposing strategic solutions.

Action Plan:

- ✓ Research Industry Trends: Stay informed about current trends and challenges in the relevant industry.
- ✓ Structured Problem-Solving: Develop a systematic approach to breaking down complex problems.
- ✓ Mock Case Studies: Practice solving case studies with peers or mentors, incorporating feedback for improvement.

Commonly Asked Interview Questions

Preparation:

Familiarity with commonly asked interview questions and having well-thought-out responses is essential. This preparation ensures you can articulate your experiences, strengths, and suitability for the role effectively.

Example: A frequently asked question is, "Tell me about yourself." A well-prepared response would include a brief overview of your professional background, key achievements, and how your skills align with the job.

Template: *"I have a [mention your academic background] and have gained [relevant experience] working at [previous company/organizations]. One of my notable achievements is [mention an accomplishment], which showcased my [key skill]. I am excited about the opportunity at [current company] because [reason]."*

Action Plan:

- ✓ Compile Common Questions: Create a list of commonly asked questions.
- ✓ Develop Responses: Craft responses that highlight your experiences, skills, and alignment with the company.
- ✓ Practice with Feedback: Conduct mock interviews to refine your responses and receive constructive feedback.

In summary, assessing your skills involves understanding the desired skills for a particular role, providing concrete examples of skill application, comprehending interview structures and stages, preparing for technical assessments and case studies, and mastering responses to commonly asked questions. By strategically preparing for these elements, candidates can confidently showcase their abilities during interviews, increasing their chances of success in securing the desired position. The subsequent chapters will build upon these foundational principles, offering deeper insights into specific interview scenarios and advanced preparation strategies.

25 Commonly Asked Interview Questions with Suggested Answers

Below is a list of 25 commonly asked interview questions along with suggested answers. Remember to tailor your responses based on your own experiences and the specific job you're applying for:

1. Tell me about yourself.
   Suggested Answer: "I have a background in [your field] with a degree in [your degree]. In my previous role at [previous company], I successfully [brief achievement]. I am passionate about [relevant aspect of your field] and am excited about the opportunity to bring my skills to this position."
2. What are your strengths?
   Suggested Answer: "One of my strengths is [specific skill], which I developed through [relevant experience]. I am also known for my [another strength], as demonstrated in my previous role where I [specific achievement]."
3. What are your weaknesses?
   Suggested Answer: "I used to struggle with [specific weakness], but I recognized it as an opportunity for growth. To address this, I [action you took to improve], and I've since seen a significant improvement in my ability to [related skill]."

4. Why do you want to work for this company?
   Suggested Answer: "I am impressed by [company's specific achievements or values], and I believe my skills align well with the company's goals. I am excited about the opportunity to contribute to [company's project/initiative] and grow professionally within this dynamic environment."
5. Describe a challenging situation at work and how you handled it.
   Suggested Answer: "In my previous role, we faced [specific challenge], affecting [outcome]. To address this, I [steps taken], collaborating with my team to implement a solution. This resulted in [positive outcome], showcasing my problem-solving and teamwork skills."
6. How do you handle stress and pressure?
   Suggested Answer: "I thrive in high-pressure situations by prioritizing tasks and maintaining a calm and focused mindset. In my previous role, during [specific stressful situation], I effectively managed my workload, ensuring deadlines were met without compromising quality."
7. What is your greatest professional achievement?
   Suggested Answer: "One of my proudest achievements is [specific achievement], where I [describe the situation, task, action, and result]. This experience not only showcased my skills but also contributed to [positive impact], highlighting my ability to make meaningful contributions."
8. Where do you see yourself in five years?

Suggested Answer: "In five years, I envision myself in a role where I have further developed my skills in [specific area] and have taken on additional responsibilities. I am committed to ongoing learning and contributing to the success of the team."

9. Why should we hire you?
   Suggested Answer: "I bring a unique combination of skills, including [mention specific skills], and a track record of [relevant achievements]. My passion for [specific aspect of the job] aligns well with the goals of the company, and I am confident that I can contribute effectively to your team."
10. How do you handle constructive criticism?
    Suggested Answer: "I view constructive criticism as an opportunity for growth. When receiving feedback, I listen actively, reflect on the comments, and identify specific actions to improve. I appreciate the chance to continuously enhance my skills and deliver better results."
11. Tell me about a time when you worked in a team.
    Suggested Answer: "In my previous role at [previous company], I was part of a cross-functional team working on [specific project]. I collaborated with team members from different departments, contributed my expertise in [your field], and together, we successfully [achievement]."
12. How do you prioritize tasks and manage your time effectively?
    Suggested Answer: "I prioritize tasks by assessing urgency and importance. I use tools

like [mention any tools or methods] to organize my schedule. In my previous role, I consistently met deadlines by effectively managing my time, resulting in the successful completion of [specific project]."

13. What motivates you?
Suggested Answer: "I am motivated by [mention specific aspects such as challenges, learning opportunities, or making a positive impact]. In my previous role, I found motivation in [specific project or accomplishment], where I could contribute my skills and see tangible results."
14. How do you handle a situation where you disagree with your supervisor?
Suggested Answer: "When faced with a disagreement, I prioritize open communication. I would respectfully express my perspective, providing supporting evidence. However, I am also open to understanding my supervisor's viewpoint. In the end, my goal is to find a mutually beneficial solution."
15. Describe a time when you had to meet a tight deadline.
Suggested Answer: "In my previous role, we had a tight deadline for [specific project]. I organized a detailed plan, allocated tasks efficiently, and communicated effectively with the team. Through our collective efforts, we not only met the deadline but also delivered a high-quality outcome."
16. How do you stay updated on industry trends?
Suggested Answer: "I stay updated on industry trends through a combination of

reading industry publications, attending relevant conferences, and participating in online forums. This continuous learning approach ensures I am aware of the latest developments in [your field]."

17. Describe a time when you had to adapt to a significant change at work.
    Suggested Answer: "At my previous job, there was a restructuring that impacted our team's workflow. I embraced the change by staying informed, seeking guidance, and adapting my working style. This flexibility allowed me to seamlessly transition and continue contributing to the team's success."
18. What is your preferred work style?
    Suggested Answer: "I have a collaborative work style, valuing open communication and teamwork. I enjoy contributing my skills while also learning from my colleagues. In my previous role, this approach fostered a positive work environment and resulted in successful team outcomes."
19. Can you provide an example of a time when you had to resolve a conflict within a team?
    Suggested Answer: "In a previous team, there was a disagreement about [specific issue]. I facilitated a constructive discussion, ensuring everyone had an opportunity to express their concerns. Through active listening and finding common ground, we resolved the conflict and strengthened team cohesion."
20. How do you ensure attention to detail in your work?
    Suggested Answer: "I maintain attention to detail by implementing a systematic approach

to tasks. I use checklists, proofreading tools, and meticulous review processes. This commitment to detail was evident in my role at [previous company], where accuracy was crucial to [specific project success]."

21. Tell me about a time when you had to deliver a presentation.

    Suggested Answer: "In my previous role, I regularly delivered presentations to [describe the audience]. For instance, I presented on [specific topic], incorporating visual aids and engaging content. This skill played a crucial role in effectively communicating complex ideas and fostering understanding."

22. How do you handle tight budgets and resource constraints?

    Suggested Answer: "I am resourceful and strategic when managing tight budgets. In a previous project with limited resources, I prioritized essential tasks, sought cost-effective solutions, and negotiated favorable terms with vendors. This approach ensured successful project completion within budget constraints."

23. What do you consider your biggest professional failure, and what did you learn from it?

    Suggested Answer: "In a past project, [describe failure], which taught me the importance of [specific lesson]. I used this experience as an opportunity for growth, implementing changes in my approach and refining my skills. The lessons learned have since contributed to my subsequent successes."

24. How do you contribute to a positive work culture?
    Suggested Answer: "I contribute to a positive work culture by fostering open communication, providing support to colleagues, and recognizing achievements. In my previous role, I initiated team-building activities and created a collaborative environment that positively impacted team morale and productivity."
25. Why did you choose [your field of study/major]?
    Suggested Answer: "I chose [your field of study/major] because of my passion for [specific aspect]. I have always been fascinated by [mention relevant topics], and pursuing this field allowed me to delve deeper into my interests. The knowledge gained has been instrumental in shaping my career path."

Remember, these are suggested answers, and it's crucial to customize your responses based on your unique experiences and the specific requirements of the job you're applying for. Additionally, practicing these responses in a mock interview setting can enhance your confidence and delivery during the actual interview.

Understanding the Human Iceberg

The "Human Iceberg" concept suggests that individuals reveal only a fraction of themselves in professional settings, much like an iceberg where only a small portion is visible above the surface. This chapter delves into handling different types of interview questions, particularly those that explore beneath the surface to assess behavioral traits, competencies, reactions to challenging situations, and creative thinking.

Handling Behavioral Interviews

Behavioral interviews focus on past behaviors as indicators of future performance. Candidates are asked to provide specific examples of how they handled situations in the past, aiming to reveal patterns of behavior and key competencies.

Example: A common behavioral question is, "Can you describe a situation where you had to resolve a conflict within your team?" This question assesses a candidate's conflict resolution skills and teamwork.

Action Plan:

- ✓ Identify Key Competencies: Review the job description to identify specific competencies sought by the employer.
- ✓ Craft STAR Stories: Develop Situation, Task, Action, Result (STAR) stories to structure your responses effectively.
- ✓ Diverse Examples: Prepare examples that showcase a range of skills, such as leadership, teamwork, and problem-solving.

Example of Behavioral Interviews with Suggested Answers

Practical Application:

Reviewing sample behavioral interview questions and suggested answers provides insights into structuring responses and showcasing relevant skills.

Sample Question: *"Tell me about a time when you had to meet a tight deadline."*

Suggested Answer: *"In my previous role at [Company], we faced a critical project deadline. I took the initiative to streamline our workflow, prioritized tasks, and communicated closely with the team. As a result, we not only met the deadline but also improved our efficiency in subsequent projects."*

Examples of Good and Poor Answers

Analyzing examples of good and poor answers helps candidates understand the qualities that interviewers appreciate and areas for improvement.

Good Answer Example: *"When faced with a challenging team project, I recognized the importance of clear communication. I initiated regular team meetings, ensuring everyone was on the same page, which significantly improved our collaboration and project outcomes."*

Poor Answer Example: *"I once had a conflict with a team member, and it didn't end well. We just couldn't agree, and the project suffered. It was frustrating, but there wasn't much I could do."*

Action Plan:

- ✓ Self-Assessment: Critically evaluate your past experiences and consider how they align with key competencies.
- ✓ Seek Feedback: Review your responses with mentors or peers to identify areas for improvement.

- ✓ Continuous Improvement: Learn from poor answers, adjusting your approach for future responses.

25 Sample Behavioral Interview Questions with Suggested Answers

Below is a list of 25 sample behavioral interview questions along with suggested answers. Behavioral questions are designed to assess how you've handled specific situations in the past, focusing on your actions, behaviors, and decision-making. Tailor your responses based on your own experiences:

1. Describe a situation where you had to meet a tight deadline.
   Suggested Answer: "In my previous role at [company], we faced a tight deadline for [specific project]. I organized a detailed plan, delegated tasks effectively, and maintained open communication with the team. Despite the pressure, we successfully met the deadline and delivered a high-quality outcome."
2. Tell me about a time when you had to work on a project with a tight budget.
   Suggested Answer: "In a previous project, we had budget constraints. I strategically allocated resources, negotiated favorable terms with vendors, and identified cost-effective solutions. This approach allowed us to complete the project within budget while maintaining quality standards."
3. Describe a situation where you had to deal with a difficult team member.
   Suggested Answer: "In my previous role, I encountered a challenging team member who

often disagreed with the team. I addressed the issue through open communication, actively listening to their concerns, and finding common ground. This collaborative approach improved team dynamics and productivity."

4. Tell me about a time when you had to adapt to a significant change at work.
   Suggested Answer: "During a restructuring at my previous company, I embraced the change by staying informed, seeking guidance, and adapting my working style. I effectively transitioned into the new structure, ensuring continuity in my responsibilities and contributing to team success."
5. Describe a situation where you had to resolve a conflict within a team.
   Suggested Answer: "In a previous team, conflict arose over [specific issue]. I facilitated a constructive discussion, ensuring everyone had an opportunity to express their concerns. Through active listening and finding common ground, we resolved the conflict, leading to strengthened team cohesion."
6. Tell me about a time when you had to deliver critical feedback to a colleague.
   Suggested Answer: "In my role as a team lead, I had to provide constructive feedback to a team member. I approached the conversation with empathy, focused on specific behaviors, and offered actionable suggestions for improvement. The feedback was well-received, and the team member showed positive growth."
7. Describe a situation where you had to handle competing priorities.

Suggested Answer: "In a previous role, I often dealt with competing priorities. I organized tasks based on urgency and importance, communicated effectively with stakeholders, and managed my time efficiently. This approach ensured all tasks were addressed, and deadlines were met."

8. Tell me about a time when you had to make a difficult decision under pressure.
   Suggested Answer: "During a crisis situation at my previous job, I had to make a critical decision under tight deadlines. I gathered relevant information, consulted with key stakeholders, and made a decision based on the best available data. The decision resulted in a positive resolution to the crisis."
9. Describe a situation where you had to take the lead on a project.
   Suggested Answer: "In my previous role, I took the lead on [specific project]. I initiated project planning, assigned tasks based on team members' strengths, and ensured effective collaboration. This leadership approach contributed to the project's success and strengthened team cohesion."
10. Tell me about a time when you had to manage a challenging client or customer.
    Suggested Answer: "During my time in customer service, I encountered a challenging client who was dissatisfied with our product. I actively listened to their concerns, empathized with their experience, and provided a solution that addressed their issues. The client's satisfaction increased, and they became a repeat customer."

11. Describe a situation where you had to think creatively to solve a problem.
    Suggested Answer: "In my role at [previous company], we faced a unique challenge where the standard solutions weren't applicable. I organized a brainstorming session, encouraged team members to think creatively, and proposed an innovative solution. This approach led to a successful resolution of the problem."
12. Tell me about a time when you had to deal with ambiguity or uncertainty.
    Suggested Answer: "During a period of organizational change at my previous job, there was uncertainty about roles and responsibilities. I proactively sought clarification from leadership, adapted to the evolving situation, and maintained focus on my goals. This flexibility contributed to a smooth transition."
13. Describe a situation where you had to influence others to adopt your ideas.
    Suggested Answer: "In a cross-functional project, I had an idea for [specific improvement]. I presented a compelling case, highlighting the benefits, and actively engaged with team members to address concerns. Through effective communication and collaboration, my idea was adopted, leading to positive outcomes."
14. Tell me about a time when you had to learn a new skill quickly.
    Suggested Answer: "In my previous role, I needed to quickly learn [specific skill] to contribute to a project. I took the initiative to

attend relevant training, sought guidance from experts, and practiced the skill consistently. This proactive approach allowed me to proficiently use the new skill within a short timeframe."

15. Describe a situation where you had to motivate a team during challenging times.
    Suggested Answer: "During a challenging project at my previous job, the team morale was low. I organized team-building activities, acknowledged individual contributions, and provided encouragement. This motivational approach boosted team spirits, leading to improved collaboration and project success."
16. Tell me about a time when you had to meet the expectations of a demanding supervisor.
    Suggested Answer: "In my role at [previous company], I had a demanding supervisor with high expectations. I consistently communicated progress, proactively addressed concerns, and delivered high-quality results. This approach not only met but exceeded the supervisor's expectations."
17. Describe a situation where you had to demonstrate resilience in the face of failure.
    Suggested Answer: "In a previous project, we faced unexpected challenges that led to setbacks. I maintained a positive mindset, learned from the experience, and implemented changes in our approach. This resilience allowed the team to overcome obstacles and ultimately succeed in the project."
18. Tell me about a time when you had to delegate tasks effectively.

Suggested Answer: "As a project manager, I had to delegate tasks for [specific project]. I assessed team members' strengths, assigned tasks accordingly, and ensured open communication throughout. This delegation strategy optimized team efficiency and contributed to the project's timely completion."

19. Describe a situation where you had to navigate a cultural or diversity-related challenge.
    Suggested Answer: "In my previous role, I worked in a diverse team where cultural differences occasionally led to misunderstandings. I actively promoted open communication, encouraged mutual understanding, and organized team-building activities. This approach fostered a positive, inclusive team culture."
20. Tell me about a time when you had to handle sensitive or confidential information.
    Suggested Answer: "In my role with [previous company], I regularly handled sensitive client information. I adhered strictly to confidentiality protocols, implemented secure data management practices, and ensured that all team members were trained on data protection measures. This approach maintained the trust of clients and stakeholders."
21. Describe a situation where you had to mentor or train a colleague.
    Suggested Answer: "In a previous role, I mentored a new team member during their onboarding process. I provided guidance on [specific tasks], shared best practices, and

ensured their smooth integration into the team. This mentoring approach contributed to the colleague's success in their role."

22. Tell me about a time when you had to make a decision without complete information.
    Suggested Answer: "In a fast-paced project, there was limited information available for a critical decision. I gathered the available data, consulted with relevant stakeholders, and made an informed decision based on the best information at the time. This approach ensured timely progress in the project."
23. Describe a situation where you had to balance multiple competing priorities.
    Suggested Answer: "During a busy period at my previous job, I had to balance multiple projects with tight deadlines. I organized tasks based on urgency, communicated effectively with stakeholders, and utilized time management tools. This approach allowed me to address all priorities efficiently."
24. Tell me about a time when you had to admit to making a mistake.
    Suggested Answer: "In a previous project, I made an error in [specific aspect]. I immediately took responsibility, communicated transparently with the team, and proposed a corrective action plan. This accountability demonstrated my commitment to continuous improvement and earned the team's trust."
25. Describe a situation where you had to lead a team through a period of change.
    Suggested Answer: "During a restructuring at my previous company, I took a leadership role in guiding my team through the changes. I

communicated openly, addressed concerns, and provided support to team members. This leadership approach contributed to a smooth transition and maintained team morale."

When responding to behavioral interview questions, use the STAR (Situation, Task, Action, Result) method to provide a structured and comprehensive answer. This ensures that you not only describe the context of the situation but also emphasize your actions and the positive outcomes achieved.

Handling Competency-Based Questions

Strategic Approach:

Competency-based questions assess specific skills and behaviors relevant to the job. Understanding how to navigate these questions is essential for demonstrating your suitability for the role.

Example: A competency-based question might be, "Can you provide an example of when you demonstrated excellent communication skills in a challenging situation?"

Action Plan:

- ✓ Review Job Competencies: Identify the competencies emphasized in the job description.
- ✓ Structured Responses: Use the STAR method to structure responses, providing clear examples of competency application.
- ✓ Tailor Responses: Customize your responses to align with the competencies valued by the company.

25 Sample Competency-based Questions along with Recommended Answers

Competency-based questions assess specific skills and behaviors relevant to the job. Below is a list of 25 sample competency-based questions along with recommended answers. Customize your responses based on your own experiences:

1. Adaptability:
   Question: "Describe a situation where you had to adapt to unexpected changes. How did you handle it?"
   Answer: "In my previous role, a sudden change in project requirements occurred. I quickly assessed the situation, adjusted project timelines, and communicated the changes to the team. This adaptability ensured minimal disruptions, and we successfully met the revised project goals."
2. Communication Skills:
   Question: "Give an example of a time when you had to communicate complex information to a non-technical audience."
   Answer: "In a cross-functional project, I had to convey technical details to a non-technical team. I used clear and concise language, visual aids, and facilitated a Q&A session to ensure everyone understood. This effective communication fostered collaboration and project success."
3. Teamwork:
   Question: "Describe a situation where you had to collaborate with individuals from different departments to achieve a common goal."
   Answer: "In a company-wide initiative, I collaborated with teams from marketing, sales,

and IT to implement a new system. I facilitated effective communication, addressed concerns, and ensured each department's needs were met. This teamwork resulted in a seamless system launch."

4. Problem-Solving:
   Question: "Give an example of a challenging problem you faced at work and how you approached solving it."
   Answer: "During a product launch, we encountered unexpected production delays. I led a problem-solving session, identified root causes, and implemented corrective actions. This proactive approach minimized the impact on the launch schedule and ensured a successful product release."
5. Leadership:
   Question: "Tell me about a time when you took on a leadership role in a project or team."
   Answer: "As a project manager, I led a team in implementing a new software system. I set clear objectives, delegated tasks based on team members' strengths, and provided guidance. This leadership approach resulted in the project's timely completion and successful implementation."
6. Initiative:
   Question: "Describe a situation where you took the initiative to improve a process or solve a problem."
   Answer: "In my role, I noticed inefficiencies in our workflow. I proactively conducted a process review, identified areas for improvement, and presented a proposal to streamline the workflow. This initiative led to

increased efficiency and a 20% reduction in project turnaround time."

7. Conflict Resolution:
   Question: "Share an example of a conflict you resolved within a team. How did you handle it?"
   Answer: "In a project team, conflicting opinions arose regarding project priorities. I facilitated a constructive discussion, encouraged open communication, and worked collaboratively to find a compromise. This conflict resolution approach strengthened team cohesion and improved overall productivity."
8. Time Management:
   Question: "Describe a situation where you had to manage multiple deadlines simultaneously."
   Answer: "In my previous role, I juggled multiple projects with tight deadlines. I prioritized tasks based on urgency, utilized time management tools, and communicated effectively with stakeholders. This time management strategy ensured all projects were completed on schedule."
9. Decision-Making:
   Question: "Tell me about a time when you had to make a difficult decision under uncertainty."
   Answer: "During a market downturn, I had to make decisions on resource allocation. I gathered relevant data, consulted with key stakeholders, and made informed decisions that positioned the company for long-term stability. This decision-making approach contributed to the company's resilience."
10. Customer Focus:

Question: "Give an example of a situation where you went above and beyond to meet a customer's needs."
Answer: "A customer expressed dissatisfaction with a product feature. I actively listened to their concerns, collaborated with the development team to implement requested changes, and provided regular updates. This customer-focused approach not only retained the customer but also improved overall product satisfaction."

11. Innovation:
    Question: "Describe a situation where you introduced an innovative idea or process in your previous role."
    Answer: "In a project, I introduced a new collaboration tool that improved communication and project tracking. I presented the benefits to the team, conducted training sessions, and monitored the implementation. This innovation enhanced team efficiency and collaboration."
12. Resilience:
    Question: "Tell me about a time when you faced setbacks or challenges at work. How did you bounce back?"
    Answer: "During a project, unexpected challenges arose that delayed our timeline. I maintained a positive mindset, gathered the team to reassess the plan, and implemented adjustments. This resilience allowed the team to overcome obstacles and ultimately succeed in the project."
13. Influencing Skills:

Question: "Share an example of a situation where you had to influence others to adopt your idea or proposal."
Answer: "In a cross-functional project, I proposed a change in the project management methodology. I presented a compelling case, highlighting the benefits, and actively engaged with team members to address concerns. Through effective communication and collaboration, my idea was adopted, leading to positive outcomes."

14. Delegation:
    Question: "Describe a situation where you effectively delegated tasks within a team or project."
    Answer: "As a team lead, I delegated tasks for a complex project. I assessed team members' strengths, communicated clear expectations, and provided necessary support. This delegation strategy optimized team efficiency and contributed to the project's successful completion."
15. Interpersonal Skills:
    Question: "How do you ensure positive working relationships with your colleagues and team members?"
    Answer: "I prioritize open communication, actively listen to others' perspectives, and value diverse opinions. I organize team-building activities to foster a positive work environment, and I am always willing to provide support and collaborate to achieve common goals."
16. Negotiation Skills:

Question: "Share an example of a situation where you had to negotiate with a vendor or external partner."
Answer: "In contract negotiations with a vendor, I identified mutual goals, conducted thorough research, and negotiated favorable terms. I ensured a win-win situation by finding common ground and maintaining a positive relationship with the vendor, which benefited both parties."

17. Attention to Detail:
    Question: "Describe a situation where your attention to detail was crucial to the success of a project."
    Answer: "During a data analysis project, attention to detail was paramount. I implemented rigorous quality checks, utilized proofreading tools, and meticulously reviewed data. This commitment to detail ensured accurate results and contributed to the overall success of the project."
18. Team Leadership:
    Question: "Tell me about a time when you provided leadership to your team during a challenging project."
    Answer: "In a high-stakes project, I provided clear direction, motivated the team, and ensured open communication. I addressed challenges promptly, recognized individual contributions, and led the team to successful project completion. This leadership approach fostered a positive team dynamic."
19. Conflict Management:

Question: "Describe a situation where you successfully managed a conflict between two team members."
Answer: "In a project team, conflict arose over differing opinions on project priorities. I facilitated a constructive discussion, actively listened to both parties, and worked collaboratively to find a resolution. This conflict management approach strengthened team relationships and improved overall collaboration."

20. Strategic Thinking:
Question: "Share an example of how you applied strategic thinking to achieve a long-term goal."
Answer: "In my role, I developed a strategic plan for [specific initiative]. I conducted a thorough analysis, identified key milestones, and aligned the plan with the company's long-term objectives. This strategic approach ensured successful implementation and contributed to the company's growth."
21. Empathy:
Question: "How do you demonstrate empathy in your interactions with colleagues or clients?"
Answer: "I actively listen to others' concerns, acknowledge different perspectives, and show understanding. In a client-facing role, I successfully resolved a complaint by empathizing with the client's experience, addressing their concerns, and ensuring a positive resolution."
22. Continuous Learning:

Question: "Describe a situation where you actively pursued learning to improve your skills or knowledge."
Answer: "In my previous role, I enrolled in relevant training courses to enhance my understanding of emerging technologies. I applied the new knowledge to optimize processes, and I shared insights with the team. This commitment to continuous learning contributed to personal and team development."

23. Customer Relationship Management:
Question: "How do you build and maintain positive relationships with customers or clients?"
Answer: "I prioritize responsiveness, address customer needs promptly, and establish trust through transparent communication. I actively seek feedback, implement improvements based on customer input, and ensure a positive customer experience."
24. Inclusivity:
Question: "Describe a situation where you promoted inclusivity and diversity in the workplace."
Answer: "I organized diversity and inclusion workshops to educate the team on the importance of inclusivity. I actively encouraged diverse voices in meetings, implemented inclusive hiring practices, and ensured a workplace environment where everyone feels valued and respected."
25. Goal Setting:
Question: "Share an example of how you set and achieved a challenging professional goal."

Answer: "I set a goal to increase team efficiency by 15% within a quarter. I developed a strategic plan, communicated clear expectations to the team, and monitored progress through key performance indicators. This goal-setting approach resulted in a 20% improvement in team efficiency."

When responding to competency-based questions, use the STAR (Situation, Task, Action, Result) method to structure your answers effectively. This ensures that you provide a comprehensive response by describing the context of the situation, the task at hand, the actions you took, and the positive results achieved.

Handling Situational Type Questions

Critical Thinking:

Situational questions assess a candidate's ability to think critically and make decisions in hypothetical scenarios. Responding effectively requires a structured and thoughtful approach.

Example: "If you were the team lead and faced with a team member not meeting deadlines, how would you handle the situation?"

Action Plan:

- ✓ Understand the Scenario: Take a moment to comprehend the scenario and key elements.
- ✓ Structured Response: Outline your thought process, consider alternative solutions, and provide a well-reasoned response.
- ✓ Emphasize Communication: Highlight the importance of open communication and collaboration in resolving the situation.

25 Examples of Handling Situational Type Questions with recommended Answers

Situational type questions assess how you would approach hypothetical scenarios in the workplace. Below is a list of 25 sample situational questions along with recommended answers. Customize your responses based on your own experiences:

1. Leadership:
   Question: "If you were assigned a leadership role in a team with conflicting opinions, how would you handle the situation?"
   Answer: "I would initiate a team meeting to understand each member's perspective, encourage open communication, and facilitate a collaborative discussion. By identifying common ground and acknowledging diverse viewpoints, I would work towards consensus and ensure everyone feels heard."
2. Conflict Resolution:
   Question: "How would you resolve a conflict between two team members who are unable to work together effectively?"
   Answer: "I would schedule a private meeting with both individuals to understand their concerns, actively listen to their perspectives, and work towards finding a resolution. If needed, I would involve a mediator or HR to ensure a fair and impartial resolution to the conflict."
3. Adaptability:
   Question: "If a major project deadline was unexpectedly moved up, how would you adapt your team's strategy to meet the new timeline?"

Answer: "I would immediately gather the team to assess the impact of the accelerated timeline. We would prioritize tasks, reallocate resources if necessary, and streamline processes to ensure the project is completed on time while maintaining quality standards."

4. Problem-Solving:
   Question: "Imagine a situation where a critical component of a project is not working as expected. How would you approach identifying and resolving the issue?"
   Answer: "I would conduct a thorough analysis to identify the root cause, collaborate with relevant experts or team members, and implement corrective actions. Communication would be key, ensuring that all stakeholders are informed of the situation, the proposed solution, and any potential impacts on the project."
5. Decision-Making:
   Question: "If you were faced with making a difficult decision that could impact your team negatively, how would you approach the decision-making process?"
   Answer: "I would gather all necessary information, consult with key stakeholders, and consider the potential outcomes and consequences of each option. Transparency in communication would be maintained, and I would make the decision that aligns with the best interests of the team and the organization."
6. Teamwork:
   Question: "Suppose you're part of a cross-functional team where members are not

collaborating effectively. How would you contribute to improving teamwork?"

Answer: "I would initiate team-building activities to foster better relationships, encourage open communication through regular meetings, and establish clear expectations for collaboration. By addressing interpersonal dynamics and promoting a positive team culture, I believe we can improve overall teamwork."

7. Customer Focus:

   Question: "If you received feedback from a customer about a product issue, how would you handle the situation to ensure customer satisfaction?"

   Answer: "I would promptly acknowledge the customer's concerns, apologize for any inconvenience, and assure them that we take their feedback seriously. I would work with the relevant teams to address the issue, provide regular updates to the customer, and offer a solution or compensation to ensure their satisfaction."

8. Time Management:

   Question: "Imagine you have multiple urgent tasks with tight deadlines. How would you prioritize and manage your time effectively to meet all deadlines?"

   Answer: "I would assess the urgency and importance of each task, create a prioritized list, and allocate time blocks for focused work. Additionally, I would communicate with stakeholders about the timelines, delegate tasks when appropriate, and regularly reassess priorities to ensure all deadlines are met."

9. Innovation:
   Question: "Suppose you were tasked with finding innovative solutions to improve a current process. How would you approach this challenge?"
   Answer: "I would conduct a thorough analysis of the current process, seek input from team members for diverse perspectives, and research industry best practices. By fostering a culture of innovation, I would encourage team members to contribute ideas, pilot new approaches, and measure the success of the implemented changes."
10. Communication Skills:
    Question: "If you were required to deliver a presentation to a diverse audience, how would you tailor your communication to ensure everyone understands the message?"
    Answer: "I would customize the content to be inclusive, using clear and straightforward language. Visual aids and examples would be incorporated to cater to different learning styles. Additionally, I would encourage questions and feedback to ensure everyone is engaged and comprehends the information."
11. Goal Setting:
    Question: "Suppose you were given a challenging project with tight deadlines. How would you set and communicate achievable goals to your team?"
    Answer: "I would break down the project into manageable tasks, set clear and realistic goals for each stage, and communicate these

goals transparently to the team. Regular check-ins and adjustments to goals based on progress would ensure that we stay on track and meet the overall project deadline."

12. Customer Relationship Management:
    Question: "If a long-standing customer expressed dissatisfaction with your company's services, how would you address the situation to retain the customer?"
    Answer: "I would reach out to the customer to understand their specific concerns, express genuine empathy, and communicate the steps we are taking to address the issues. Offering personalized solutions, such as discounts or additional support, would demonstrate our commitment to customer satisfaction."
13. Continuous Learning:
    Question: "Suppose you were assigned a new project that required skills you currently do not possess. How would you go about acquiring those skills quickly?"
    Answer: "I would proactively seek relevant training, leverage online resources, and connect with experts or colleagues who possess the necessary skills. By immersing myself in the learning process, I would acquire the required skills efficiently and contribute effectively to the success of the project."
14. Delegation:
    Question: "Imagine you were leading a large project with multiple team members. How would you delegate tasks to ensure efficiency and team engagement?"
    Answer: "I would assess each team member's strengths and expertise, delegate tasks

accordingly, and provide clear instructions and expectations. Regular check-ins, feedback sessions, and recognizing individual contributions would ensure that each team member is engaged and contributing effectively."

15. Strategic Thinking:
    Question: "If you were asked to develop a long-term strategy for your department, how would you approach the strategic thinking process?"
    Answer: "I would conduct a comprehensive analysis of the current state, identify key goals and objectives, and align them with the overall organizational strategy. Collaboration with key stakeholders, regular reassessment of the strategy, and flexibility in adapting to changes would ensure its success."
16. Resilience:
    Question: "Suppose you encountered unexpected setbacks in a project. How would you maintain team morale and drive the project to success?"
    Answer: "I would openly communicate about the setbacks, assure the team that challenges are a natural part of any project, and emphasize the importance of resilience. Encouraging a positive mindset, recognizing small victories, and offering additional support when needed would help maintain team morale."
17. Empathy:
    Question: "Imagine a team member is going through a challenging personal situation. How

would you demonstrate empathy and support in the workplace?"

Answer: "I would initiate a private conversation to express understanding and empathy, offering support or flexibility if needed. Additionally, I would maintain open communication, respect the individual's privacy, and provide resources or assistance to help them navigate through the challenging situation."

18. Negotiation Skills:

    Question: "Suppose you were negotiating a contract with a vendor, and they were resistant to certain terms. How would you handle the negotiation to reach a mutually beneficial agreement?"

    Answer: "I would focus on understanding the vendor's concerns, presenting data or evidence to support our proposed terms, and actively listening to their perspective. By finding common ground and proposing compromises when appropriate, I would work towards a mutually beneficial agreement that aligns with both parties' interests."

19. Attention to Detail:

    Question: "If you were overseeing a project where details were critical to success, how would you ensure a high level of attention to detail from your team?"

    Answer: "I would establish clear expectations regarding the importance of attention to detail, provide training on quality standards, and implement thorough quality checks throughout the project. Regular feedback sessions and recognizing meticulous work would reinforce the value of attention to detail within the team."

20. Interpersonal Skills:

    Question: "Imagine a situation where there is tension among team members. How would you use your interpersonal skills to address and resolve the tension?"

    Answer: "I would schedule a team-building session to address the tension openly, encourage team members to share their perspectives, and facilitate a constructive discussion to identify common ground. Establishing a positive team culture, celebrating achievements, and addressing concerns proactively would contribute to improved interpersonal dynamics."

21. Inclusivity:

    Question: "Suppose you noticed that certain team members are not included in decision-making processes. How would you promote inclusivity within the team?"

    Answer: "I would actively seek input from all team members, ensure diverse voices are heard during meetings, and provide opportunities for contributions from everyone. Addressing any barriers to participation and fostering an inclusive environment where everyone feels valued and respected would be a priority."

22. Influencing Skills:

    Question: "If you were tasked with introducing a new idea to your team, and there was resistance, how would you use your influencing skills to gain support?"

Answer: "I would present a compelling case for the idea, emphasizing its benefits and aligning it with the team's goals. Actively seeking input, addressing concerns, and incorporating team members' feedback would demonstrate a collaborative approach, ultimately gaining support for the new idea."

23. Team Leadership:
    Question: "Suppose you were leading a team through a challenging project, and morale was low. How would you provide effective leadership to boost team morale and motivation?"
    Answer: "I would openly address the low morale, acknowledge the challenges, and emphasize the importance of the team's contributions. Implementing morale-boosting activities, recognizing individual and team achievements, and actively supporting the team through challenges would contribute to improved morale and motivation."
24. Continuous Learning:
    Question: "Imagine you were assigned to a project that required knowledge of a new technology. How would you approach learning and incorporating this new technology into the project?"
    Answer: "I would enroll in relevant training, seek guidance from experts or online resources, and apply the knowledge through hands-on experience. Regular updates to the team, sharing insights, and encouraging collaborative learning would ensure a smooth integration of the new technology into the project."

25. Goal Setting:
    Question: "Suppose you were given a project with ambiguous goals. How would you work with the team to define clear and achievable objectives?"
    Answer: "I would initiate a collaborative goal-setting session with the team, encouraging input from all members. By defining specific, measurable, and realistic goals, we would establish a shared understanding of the project's objectives. Regular check-ins and adjustments based on progress would ensure we stay on course."

When responding to situational questions, use the STAR (Situation, Task, Action, Result) method to structure your answers effectively. This ensures that you provide a comprehensive response by describing the context of the situation, the task at hand, the actions you took, and the positive results achieved.

Handling Creative Questions

Innovation:

Creative questions assess a candidate's ability to think outside the box and approach challenges with innovative solutions. Responding to these questions requires a balance of creativity and practicality.

Example: "If you were given unlimited resources, how would you improve the efficiency of our current processes?"

Action Plan:

- ✓ Creativity and Practicality: Blend creative ideas with practical considerations for implementation.

- ✓ Demonstrate Value: Emphasize how your proposed solution aligns with the company's goals and values.
- ✓ Consider Multiple Perspectives: Anticipate potential challenges or considerations and address them in your response.

25 Examples of Handling Creative Questions with recommended Answers

Creative questions are designed to assess your ability to think outside the box and approach challenges with innovative solutions. Below is a list of 25 sample creative questions along with recommended answers. Remember to tailor your responses based on your own experiences and the specific context of the question:

1. Question: "If you were a product, what features would you have, and how would you market yourself?"
   Answer: "As a product, I would emphasize versatility, adaptability, and a user-friendly interface. I would market myself through engaging storytelling, showcasing real-life scenarios where I bring value and solve problems for users."
2. Question: "Imagine you have a magic wand. What three things would you change about the traditional interview process, and why?"
   Answer: "I would streamline communication between candidates and employers, incorporate interactive elements to showcase practical skills, and implement ongoing feedback loops to ensure continuous improvement and a more positive candidate experience."

3. Question: "If you were asked to redesign a popular social media platform, what new features or improvements would you introduce?"
   Answer: "I would focus on enhancing user privacy, implementing advanced content moderation algorithms, and introducing features that promote meaningful connections and community engagement while minimizing the negative aspects often associated with social media."
4. Question: "If you were given the task of organizing a team-building event, what creative and inclusive activities would you plan?"
   Answer: "I would organize a 'Collaborative Innovation Challenge' where teams work together to solve real-world problems. This not only fosters teamwork but also allows individuals to showcase their creativity, problem-solving, and communication skills."
5. Question: "Imagine you are a superhero. What unique skills or powers do you possess, and how would you use them to benefit your workplace?"
   Answer: "As the 'Innovator,' my superpower would be to generate creative solutions effortlessly. I would use this power to inspire my team, overcome challenges, and contribute to a culture of continuous improvement and forward-thinking."
6. Question: "If you were tasked with creating a mascot for your university, what would it be, and what qualities would it represent?"

Answer: "I would create a mascot named 'Pioneer Pride,' symbolizing innovation, resilience, and a commitment to exploring new frontiers. This mascot would embody the spirit of the university's students as trailblazers in their academic and professional journeys."

7. Question: "Imagine you have a time machine. Which historical figure would you bring to the present day, and how would they contribute to your team?"

   Answer: "I would bring Leonardo da Vinci for his multidisciplinary genius. His ability to merge art, science, and innovation would inspire a culture of interdisciplinary collaboration, creativity, and out-of-the-box thinking within the team."

8. Question: "If you were given a budget to create an employee wellness program, what creative initiatives would you include to promote a healthy and positive work environment?"

   Answer: "I would implement 'Wellness Wednesdays,' offering activities like yoga, mindfulness sessions, and healthy cooking classes. Additionally, I would introduce a wellness challenge with personalized goals, fostering a supportive community and promoting overall well-being."

9. Question: "Imagine you are the architect of a new office space. What innovative design elements would you incorporate to enhance collaboration and productivity?"

   Answer: "I would prioritize an open and flexible layout, incorporate collaborative zones with comfortable seating, and integrate technology-driven solutions like smart whiteboards and virtual collaboration tools to facilitate seamless communication and creativity."

10. Question: "If you were to create a TED Talk, what would be your topic, and how would you engage the audience?"
    Answer: "My TED Talk would focus on 'The Power of Embracing Change.' I would share personal anecdotes, incorporate interactive elements like audience polls, and use visuals to convey a compelling narrative that inspires individuals to embrace change as a catalyst for growth."
11. Question: "Imagine you are given the opportunity to organize a company-wide innovation competition. What guidelines and criteria would you establish to encourage creativity and diverse ideas?"
    Answer: "I would encourage participants to address real business challenges, prioritize inclusivity and diversity of thought, and evaluate submissions based on innovation, feasibility, and potential impact. Providing mentorship and resources would further foster a culture of innovation."
12. Question: "If you were to design a smartphone app to enhance workplace communication, what features would it include, and how would it benefit the team?"
    Answer: "The app, 'TeamConnect,' would include features like instant messaging, project collaboration boards, and virtual team-building activities. It aims to streamline communication, foster collaboration, and

enhance team cohesion by providing a centralized platform for information sharing and engagement."

13. Question: "Imagine you are the director of a documentary about the future of work. What themes and perspectives would you explore to capture the essence of evolving work environments?"

    Answer: "I would explore themes of remote work, artificial intelligence, and the changing nature of leadership. Through interviews with thought leaders, employees, and experts, the documentary would provide a comprehensive view of how work is evolving and the challenges and opportunities it presents."

14. Question: "If you were tasked with organizing a company-wide 'Innovation Day,' what activities and events would you plan to inspire creativity and collaboration among employees?"

    Answer: "I would organize design thinking workshops, guest speaker sessions from industry innovators, and a company-wide ideation challenge. These activities would encourage employees to explore new ideas, collaborate across departments, and contribute to a culture of continuous innovation."

15. Question: "Imagine you have the ability to implement a 'Future Skills Training Program' for your team. What skills would you prioritize, and how would you ensure successful implementation?"

    Answer: "I would prioritize skills such as adaptability, critical thinking, and digital literacy. The program would include hands-on workshops, mentorship opportunities, and continuous learning platforms to ensure that team members acquire and apply these future-ready skills in their roles."

16. Question: "If you were to organize a team-building retreat, what location and activities would you choose to promote team bonding and creativity?"
    Answer: "I would choose a scenic location with opportunities for outdoor activities, team-building exercises, and creative workshops. The retreat would include activities like hiking, brainstorming sessions in natural settings, and collaborative projects to strengthen team bonds and foster creativity."
17. Question: "Imagine you have the chance to redesign your company's logo. What elements would you incorporate to reflect the organization's values and vision?"
    Answer: "I would incorporate modern design elements, vibrant colors, and symbolic imagery that represents the company's commitment to innovation, inclusivity, and sustainability. The redesigned logo would aim to visually convey the essence of the organization to both internal and external stakeholders."
18. Question: "If you were given the opportunity to curate a company-wide art exhibition, what themes and artworks would you choose to inspire creativity and conversation among employees?"
    Answer: "I would choose themes like 'Innovation in Diversity' and 'The Power of

Collaboration.' The artworks would range from traditional paintings to digital art, showcasing diverse perspectives and inspiring dialogue among employees about the importance of creativity and collaboration in the workplace."

19. Question: "Imagine you have the chance to create a unique employee recognition program. What creative incentives and rewards would you implement to acknowledge outstanding contributions?"

    Answer: "I would introduce personalized 'Innovation Awards' that recognize employees for their creative problem-solving, collaboration, and impact. In addition to traditional rewards, recipients would have the opportunity to showcase their achievements through company-wide presentations and leadership recognition."

20. Question: "If you were to design a board game that reflects the dynamics of a successful team, what elements and challenges would you include to make it both fun and educational?"

    Answer: "The board game, 'Team Triumph,' would include challenges related to communication, problem-solving, and strategic planning. By navigating these challenges, players would learn valuable teamwork skills and experience the importance of collaboration in achieving shared goals."

21. Question: "Imagine you were asked to create a viral social media campaign to promote workplace diversity and inclusion. What creative content and strategies would you employ to make a meaningful impact?"

Answer: "I would create engaging video content featuring diverse employee stories, host live Q&A sessions with diversity advocates, and encourage employees to share their experiences. The campaign would leverage social media trends to amplify the message and foster a culture of inclusivity within the organization."

22. Question: "If you had the opportunity to design a company-wide innovation challenge, what problem statement would you present to employees, and how would you encourage diverse solutions?"

    Answer: "The challenge would focus on improving sustainability in daily operations. I would encourage diverse solutions by emphasizing the importance of cross-functional collaboration, providing resources for research, and organizing ideation sessions to spark creative thinking across departments."

23. Question: "Imagine you were tasked with creating a podcast series for your company. What topics and formats would you choose to engage employees and promote a culture of continuous learning?"

    Answer: "The podcast series, 'Innovation Insights,' would cover topics such as emerging industry trends, employee spotlights, and interviews with thought leaders. The format would include a mix of informative discussions, storytelling, and actionable takeaways to inspire continuous learning and curiosity among employees."

24. Question: "If you were given the responsibility of designing an interactive onboarding experience for new employees, what elements and activities would you include to welcome them to the company culture?"
Answer: "The onboarding experience would include virtual reality tours, interactive quizzes about company values, and virtual meet-and-greet sessions with key team members. These elements would immerse new employees in the company culture, making the onboarding process informative, engaging, and memorable."
25. Question: "Imagine you were asked to create a 'Future Workspaces' initiative. What innovative design features and technologies would you incorporate to enhance the physical and virtual work environment?"
Answer: "I would incorporate flexible and ergonomic workstations, collaborative spaces with smart technology, and virtual reality meeting rooms. This initiative would aim to provide employees with a dynamic and adaptable work environment that fosters creativity, collaboration, and productivity."

When responding to creative questions, demonstrate your ability to think innovatively, consider diverse perspectives, and articulate your ideas in a clear and compelling manner.

Responding to Challenging Questions

Resilience:

Challenging questions may aim to assess how well candidates handle pressure, ambiguity, or ethical dilemmas. Responding effectively requires composure, transparency, and an ethical standpoint. Example: "How do you handle criticism, and can you provide an example of a situation where you received feedback and implemented positive changes?"

Action Plan:

- ✓ Acknowledge Feedback: Demonstrate a willingness to receive constructive criticism.
- ✓ Highlight Growth: Share an example where you implemented feedback to showcase continuous improvement.
- ✓ Maintain Professionalism: Respond to challenging questions with composure and a positive attitude.

10 Examples of Challenging Questions with Suggested Answers

Challenging questions are designed to test your ability to handle difficult situations and demonstrate resilience, critical thinking, and problem-solving skills. Here are 10 sample challenging questions along with recommended answers:

1. Question: "Describe a situation where you faced a significant setback or failure. How did you handle it, and what did you learn from the experience?"
   Answer: "In a previous project, unforeseen challenges led to a missed deadline. I took immediate responsibility, communicated transparently with the team, and initiated a comprehensive analysis of the issues. By learning from the experience, we implemented new project management strategies, leading to improved outcomes in subsequent projects."

2. Question: "If you were working on a team project, and a team member consistently underperformed, how would you address the situation?"
   Answer: "I would initiate a private conversation with the team member to understand any underlying challenges they may be facing. If performance issues persisted, I would involve the team lead or manager to explore supportive measures, such as additional training or reassignment of tasks, to ensure the overall success of the project."
3. Question: "How do you handle criticism, especially when it is unwarranted or delivered in a harsh manner?"
   Answer: "I approach criticism as an opportunity for growth. I actively listen to the feedback, separate emotions from the message, and focus on the constructive aspects. If criticism is delivered harshly, I remain composed and seek clarification on specific points to better understand the concerns. I use the feedback to continually improve my skills and performance."
4. Question: "Tell me about a time when you had to navigate a conflicting situation between team members. How did you resolve the conflict?"
   Answer: "I facilitated a team discussion to identify the root causes of the conflict, encouraged open communication, and helped the team members find common ground. By addressing individual concerns and fostering a collaborative environment, we were able to

resolve the conflict, improve communication, and strengthen team dynamics."

5. Question: "If you disagreed with a decision made by your supervisor, how would you express your dissent while maintaining a positive working relationship?"
   Answer: "I would approach the situation respectfully, expressing my perspective with clear and well-reasoned arguments. I would seek to understand the reasoning behind the decision and propose alternative solutions that align with the team's goals. It's essential to communicate professionally and contribute constructively to decision-making processes."
6. Question: "Describe a situation where you had to meet a tight deadline with limited resources. How did you prioritize tasks and ensure successful completion of the project?"
   Answer: "In a previous role, I faced a tight deadline with limited resources. I prioritized tasks based on their impact on project success, leveraged existing resources efficiently, and communicated transparently with the team about the constraints. Through strategic planning and collaboration, we successfully met the deadline and achieved project objectives."
7. Question: "If a project you were leading was not meeting expectations, how would you identify the issues and implement corrective actions?"
   Answer: "I would conduct a thorough project review to identify areas of concern, gather feedback from team members, and assess the project against initial goals. Based on the

findings, I would develop a corrective action plan, reallocate resources if necessary, and communicate transparently with stakeholders. The key is to proactively address issues and course-correct to ensure project success."

8. Question: "How do you handle competing priorities and tight deadlines without compromising the quality of your work?"
   Answer: "I prioritize tasks based on urgency and impact, delegate when possible, and use effective time management techniques. While meeting deadlines is crucial, I emphasize maintaining a high standard of work by setting realistic expectations, communicating with stakeholders about timelines, and delivering results that meet or exceed expectations."
9. Question: "Describe a situation where you faced resistance while implementing a new idea or process. How did you overcome the resistance and drive successful implementation?"
   Answer: "I initiated open communication to understand concerns, presented a compelling case for the new idea, and actively sought input from team members. By addressing specific concerns, providing data to support the change, and involving the team in decision-making, we successfully navigated resistance and achieved successful implementation."
10. Question: "If you were assigned a project outside your area of expertise, how would you approach the learning curve and ensure successful project delivery?"

Answer: "I would embrace the opportunity as a chance for professional growth. I would proactively seek relevant training, leverage the expertise of team members, and conduct thorough research to quickly acquire the necessary knowledge. Regular check-ins and collaboration with experienced colleagues would ensure I meet the project requirements and contribute effectively."

When responding to challenging questions, emphasize your ability to remain composed under pressure, problem-solving skills, and your commitment to continuous improvement. Tailor your answers to showcase your specific experiences and achievements in overcoming challenging situations.

In conclusion, understanding the human iceberg involves navigating behavioral interviews, providing sample responses, evaluating good and poor answers, addressing competency-based and situational questions, tackling creative inquiries, and responding to challenging questions with resilience. Mastering this aspect of the interview process ensures candidates can reveal the depth of their capabilities and align with the company's values and expectations. The subsequent chapters will further explore advanced strategies and scenarios to enhance your interview preparedness.

Practicing Your Interview

Strategies for Effective Interview Practice

Effective interview practice is a crucial step in preparing for actual interviews. It involves simulating real interview scenarios, refining responses, and enhancing overall performance.

Example: Consider a scenario where a candidate is preparing for a marketing position. Effective practice involves researching industry-specific questions, creating tailored responses, and practicing articulating ideas clearly and concisely.

Action Plan:

- ✓ Understand the Job Requirements: Analyze the job description to identify key skills and competencies.
- ✓ Create a Question Bank: Develop a list of potential interview questions relevant to the role.
- ✓ Simulate Real Conditions: Practice in an environment similar to an actual interview, including dressing professionally and using interview-appropriate body language.

Mock Interviews and Feedback

Practical Application:

Conducting mock interviews with a mentor, career advisor, or a trusted friend provides valuable feedback and helps candidates identify areas for improvement.

Example: During a mock interview, a candidate may receive feedback on the clarity of their responses, body language, and the overall structure of their answers.

Action Plan:

- ✓ Choose a Trusted Partner: Select someone who can provide constructive and honest feedback.
- ✓ Use Interview Platforms: Utilize online platforms offering mock interview simulations and feedback.
- ✓ Record and Review: Record mock interviews to review your performance objectively and identify areas for improvement.

Tips for Verbal and Non-Verbal Communication

Effective verbal and non-verbal communication is essential in creating a positive impression during interviews. This includes articulating thoughts clearly, maintaining good eye contact, and using appropriate gestures.

Example: A candidate with strong communication skills can convey complex ideas succinctly, showcasing their ability to express thoughts coherently and persuasively.

Action Plan:

- ✓ Practice Articulation: Practice answering questions concisely and clearly to avoid rambling.
- ✓ Eye Contact and Body Language: Maintain eye contact to convey confidence and use open and positive body language.
- ✓ Pitch and Tone: Pay attention to your pitch and tone to ensure a confident and engaging delivery.

Tips for Virtual and Telephone Interviews

Remote Interviewing:

Virtual and telephone interviews present unique challenges, requiring additional considerations for effective communication and engagement.

Example: In a virtual interview, a candidate needs to be mindful of their background, camera angle, and the clarity of their voice to ensure a professional and distraction-free experience.

Action Plan:

- ✓ Test Technology in Advance: Ensure your camera, microphone, and internet connection are reliable.
- ✓ Choose a Quiet Environment: Minimize background noise and choose a well-lit, clutter-free space.
- ✓ Dress Professionally: Even for virtual interviews, dress professionally to convey a polished image.

Practicing for interviews is a dynamic process that involves strategic preparation, realistic simulations, and continuous refinement. By engaging in mock interviews, seeking constructive feedback, honing communication skills, and adapting to the nuances of virtual and telephone interviews, candidates can build confidence and enhance their overall interview performance.

Interest, Motivation, and Commitment

Demonstrating Passion for the Subject

Importance of Passion:

Demonstrating genuine passion for the subject matter not only showcases enthusiasm but also indicates a long-term commitment to continuous learning and growth within the field.

Example: Suppose you are interviewing for a role in environmental sustainability. Expressing a deep interest in sustainable practices, providing examples of personal initiatives, and linking these to the company's goals can demonstrate a genuine passion for the subject.

Action Plan:

- ✓ Identify Personal Connection: Reflect on personal experiences that sparked your interest in the subject.
- ✓ Highlight Relevant Experiences: Share specific instances where your passion translated into meaningful contributions or achievements.
- ✓ Connect with Company Values: Align your passion with the company's mission and values, emphasizing how your interests align with the role.

Answering Questions about Working with Others and in Teams

Teamwork and Collaboration:

Employers often seek candidates who can effectively collaborate with others. Answering questions about teamwork requires showcasing interpersonal skills, communication, and adaptability.

Example: If asked, "Describe a situation where you worked successfully in a team," share a story that highlights your ability to collaborate, resolve conflicts, and contribute to a positive team dynamic.

Template: *"In my previous role at [Company], I was part of a cross-functional team working on [specific project]. Despite differing opinions, we established open communication channels, leveraged each team member's strengths, and successfully delivered the project ahead of schedule."*

Action Plan:

- ✓ Reflect on Past Collaborations: Identify instances where you effectively collaborated with others.
- ✓ Highlight Individual Contributions: Emphasize how your unique skills positively contributed to team outcomes.
- ✓ Acknowledge Challenges: Briefly mention any challenges faced and demonstrate your problem-solving skills in addressing them.

10 Examples of Questions about Working with Others and in Teams along with Suggested Answers

Questions about working with others and in teams assess your ability to collaborate, communicate, and contribute effectively in a group setting. Here are 10 sample questions along with recommended answers:

1. Question: "Describe a situation where you had to work closely with a diverse group of individuals to achieve a common goal. What role did you play, and how did you contribute to the team's success?"

Answer: "In a previous project, I collaborated with team members from different departments with diverse skill sets. As the project manager, I facilitated effective communication, identified each team member's strengths, and allocated tasks accordingly. By fostering a collaborative environment and leveraging individual expertise, we successfully achieved our project objectives."

2. Question: "How do you handle conflicts within a team, and can you provide an example of a successful resolution you facilitated?"
   Answer: "I approach conflicts by addressing them proactively. In a previous team, I identified the underlying issues, facilitated an open discussion, and encouraged team members to express their perspectives. By finding common ground and implementing solutions collaboratively, we resolved the conflict, strengthened team relationships, and maintained a positive working environment."
3. Question: "If you were leading a team project, how would you ensure effective communication and collaboration among team members, especially when working remotely?"
   Answer: "In a remote work scenario, I would establish clear communication channels, schedule regular virtual meetings, and utilize collaboration tools to keep everyone connected. Setting expectations, providing regular updates, and fostering an inclusive environment for virtual collaboration would ensure the team remains aligned and engaged."

4. Question: "Describe a challenging situation where you had to motivate and inspire your team to overcome obstacles. How did you approach leadership in this scenario?"
   Answer: "During a tight deadline, I motivated the team by emphasizing the importance of our collective efforts and recognizing individual contributions. I led by example, demonstrated a positive attitude, and provided support where needed. By fostering a sense of camaraderie and purpose, we successfully navigated challenges and achieved our goals."
5. Question: "In a team setting, how do you ensure that all team members have an opportunity to contribute their ideas and opinions?"
   Answer: "I prioritize inclusivity by actively soliciting input from all team members during meetings, encouraging diverse perspectives, and creating an open forum for idea-sharing. By recognizing and valuing each team member's contributions, we ensure that the team benefits from a broad range of insights and experiences."
6. Question: "If you were part of a team facing a tight deadline, and one team member was struggling to keep up, how would you handle the situation to ensure the project's success?"
   Answer: "I would approach the team member privately to understand their challenges and provide support or additional resources. Simultaneously, I would assess the overall workload, redistribute tasks if necessary, and facilitate collaboration to ensure that everyone

can contribute effectively. The key is to maintain open communication and address challenges proactively."

7. Question: "How do you handle disagreements or differing opinions within a team, and how do you work towards consensus?"

   Answer: "I approach disagreements by promoting open dialogue, actively listening to varying perspectives, and seeking common ground. To work towards consensus, I encourage compromise, find solutions that align with team goals, and emphasize the importance of collaboration. By fostering a culture of respect and cooperation, we can navigate differences effectively."

8. Question: "Describe a situation where you had to delegate tasks within a team. How did you ensure that each team member's strengths were maximized, and how did you monitor progress?"

   Answer: "When delegating tasks, I assessed each team member's strengths and assigned responsibilities accordingly. Regular check-ins, clear communication of expectations, and providing necessary resources ensured that the team remained on track. By recognizing and utilizing individual strengths, we optimized performance and achieved our collective objectives."

9. Question: "If you were part of a team where members had conflicting priorities, how would you coordinate and prioritize tasks to meet overall project deadlines?"

   Answer: "I would initiate a team discussion to understand individual priorities, align goals, and collectively prioritize tasks based on project deadlines. By fostering transparency, negotiating timelines, and finding common ground, we can ensure that everyone's priorities are considered, and the team can work cohesively towards shared objectives."

10. Question: "How do you contribute to creating a positive team culture, and can you provide an example of a team achievement that highlights your collaborative approach?"
    Answer: "I contribute to a positive team culture by promoting open communication, recognizing achievements, and fostering a sense of camaraderie. In a previous project, our team achieved a significant milestone. I attribute our success to effective collaboration, clear communication, and a supportive team culture where everyone felt valued and motivated to contribute their best."

When responding to questions about working with others and in teams, emphasize your ability to communicate effectively, lead collaboratively, and contribute to a positive team dynamic. Share specific examples from your experiences to illustrate your skills and approach in team settings.

Understanding Psychometric Tests and Assessments

Psychometric tests assess cognitive abilities, personality traits, and other psychological factors. Understanding these assessments is crucial, as many employers use them as part of the hiring process.

Example: A company may use a personality test to assess a candidate's traits and determine their compatibility with the organizational culture. Familiarizing yourself with common psychometric test formats can enhance your preparedness.

Action Plan:

- ✓ Research Common Test Types: Explore common psychometric tests, such as personality assessments, aptitude tests, and situational judgment tests.
- ✓ Practice Sample Tests: Utilize online resources that offer sample psychometric tests to familiarize yourself with the format and types of questions.
- ✓ Understand the Purpose: Recognize that psychometric tests aim to provide a comprehensive understanding of your abilities, personality, and work style.
- ✓ Conclusion:
- ✓ Effectively conveying interest, motivation, and commitment during an interview involves authentically expressing your passion for the subject matter, articulating your teamwork and collaboration skills through real-world examples, and understanding the role of psychometric tests in the hiring process.

By aligning your personal interests with the company's values, showcasing your ability to collaborate and contribute to team success, and preparing for potential psychometric assessments, you position yourself as a candidate who is not only qualified but also deeply committed to the company's mission and culture.

In summary, this chapter provides insights into how candidates can effectively communicate their passion, teamwork skills, and understanding of psychometric assessments to leave a lasting impression on interviewers. The subsequent chapters will further explore advanced strategies and scenarios to elevate your interview preparedness.

When Closing the Interview

Questions to Ask Interviewers

Importance of Asking Questions:

Closing the interview with thoughtful and well-researched questions not only demonstrates your genuine interest but also allows you to gather valuable information to make an informed decision about the role and company.

Example: *"I'm very interested in the company culture. Can you share more about the team dynamics and how employees collaborate here?"*

Action Plan:

- ✓ Research the Company: Prepare questions based on your research about the company, its culture, and the role.
- ✓ Tailor Questions: Customize your questions to the specific interviewer, considering their role and experience.
- ✓ Show Enthusiasm: Express genuine interest by asking questions that go beyond basic information available on the company's website.

Asking Thoughtful Questions at the End

Asking thoughtful questions during an interview not only demonstrates your genuine interest in the position but also provides you with valuable insights into the company and role. Here are 10 sample questions to ask interviewers along with recommended answers:

1. Question: "Can you describe the team dynamic within the department?"

Answer: "Understanding the team dynamic is crucial to my success. Can you provide insights into how the team collaborates, communicates, and supports one another?"

2. Question: "What opportunities for professional development does the company offer?"
   Answer: "I value continuous learning. Could you share more about the professional development opportunities available within the company, such as training programs, mentorship, or skill-building initiatives?"
3. Question: "How would you describe the company culture, and what characteristics do you believe contribute to a successful employee in this environment?"
   Answer: "Company culture is important to me. Can you elaborate on the values and characteristics that are highly regarded here, and how they contribute to both individual and collective success?"
4. Question: "What are the key priorities for this role in the first six months, and how would success be measured?"
   Answer: "Understanding the expectations for success is crucial. Could you provide insights into the key priorities for this role in the initial six months and the metrics used to evaluate performance?"
5. Question: "How does the company foster diversity and inclusion, and what initiatives are in place to ensure an inclusive workplace?"
   Answer: "Diversity and inclusion are important aspects of a company. Can you share more about the initiatives in place to foster diversity and create an inclusive work environment?"

6. Question: "What do you enjoy most about working for this company, and how has your own career progressed here?"
   Answer: "I believe in gaining perspectives from current employees. What do you find most rewarding about working here, and how has your own career evolved within the company?"
7. Question: "How does the company encourage innovation and creative thinking among its employees?"
   Answer: "Innovation is important to me. Could you provide insights into how the company fosters a culture of creativity and encourages employees to contribute innovative ideas?"
8. Question: "What challenges or opportunities do you foresee for the department in the coming year, and how does the team typically address challenges?"
   Answer: "Understanding the current landscape is crucial. Can you discuss the challenges and opportunities you anticipate for the department in the next year and how the team typically addresses challenges collaboratively?"
9. Question: "How would you describe the leadership style within the organization, particularly within this department?"
   Answer: "Understanding the leadership style is important for alignment. Can you provide insights into the leadership style within the organization, especially within this department?"

10. Question: "What is the next step in the interview process, and when can I expect to hear back regarding the hiring decision?"
    Answer: "Expressing eagerness and timeline expectations is key. What is the next step in the interview process, and when can I anticipate receiving feedback on the hiring decision?"

Remember to tailor your questions based on the specific context of the interview and the information you've gathered during the conversation. Asking thoughtful questions not only showcases your interest but also helps you make informed decisions about whether the company and role align with your career goals.

What Questions Never to Ask?

Avoiding Red Flags:

Certain questions can potentially raise concerns or create a negative impression. It's essential to avoid questions that may be perceived as unprofessional, disrespectful, or indicative of a lack of preparedness.

Example: *"How much vacation time do I get, and can I work from home whenever I want?"*

Action Plan:

- ✓ Review Common Red Flags: Familiarize yourself with questions that may be inappropriate or premature.
- ✓ Focus on Professional Growth: Frame questions around your professional development, company goals, and expectations.
- ✓ Timing Matters: Save questions about benefits, salary, or specific details for later

stages of the hiring process, such as during negotiations.

Examples of Questions Never to Ask

While it's essential to ask thoughtful questions during an interview, there are certain topics that should be avoided as they may be inappropriate or could potentially harm your chances of securing the position. Here are 10 sample questions of what NEVER to ask interviewers:

1. Question: "What does the company do?"
   Why not to ask: This question indicates a lack of basic research about the company, which may suggest a lack of genuine interest in the role.
2. Question: "How much does this job pay, and what are the benefits?"
   Why not to ask: Salary and benefits discussions are typically reserved for later stages of the interview process or salary negotiation. Asking too early may give the impression that your main motivation is compensation.
3. Question: "How soon can I expect a promotion or salary increase?"
   Why not to ask: This question may be perceived as overly ambitious or presumptive, especially before demonstrating your skills and contributions to the company.
4. Question: "Can I work from home most of the time?"
   Why not to ask: While remote work is becoming more common, discussing this too early in the interview process may signal that you prioritize flexibility over the job itself.

5. Question: "How many vacation days do I get, and can I take extended leave?"
   Why not to ask: Questions about time off may convey a lack of commitment to the job or an expectation for significant time away from work.
6. Question: "Do you monitor employees' social media accounts?"
   Why not to ask: This question may raise concerns about privacy and professionalism. It's generally not advisable to inquire about the company's social media policies during an interview.
7. Question: "Can I change my work hours or have a flexible schedule?"
   Why not to ask: Similar to the remote work question, discussions about scheduling flexibility are better suited for later stages of the hiring process.
8. Question: "Is there a drug testing policy, and are there any substances I cannot use?"
   Why not to ask: Questions about drug testing or substance use policies may be seen as unprofessional and unrelated to the job at hand.
9. Question: "How strict is the dress code, and can I wear casual attire regularly?"
   Why not to ask: Dress code inquiries should be approached carefully. It's better to err on the side of professionalism during the interview stage and address dress code policies later, if necessary.
10. Question: "Can you tell me about the turnover rate in the company?"

Why not to ask: This question may imply concerns about job stability or create a negative impression. It's better to focus on positive aspects of the company culture and opportunities for growth.

Remember that the interview is an opportunity to showcase your qualifications and enthusiasm for the role. Avoid questions that may raise red flags or give the impression that you are primarily concerned with personal benefits rather than contributing to the success of the organization.

Handling Strength-Based Questions

Leveraging Strengths:

Strength-based questions aim to identify and assess a candidate's inherent strengths, focusing on what they enjoy and excel at. Responding effectively requires self-awareness and the ability to align personal strengths with the requirements of the role.

Example: *"Can you share an example of when you felt particularly energized and motivated at work? What aspects of the task or project fueled your enthusiasm?"*

Action Plan:

- ✓ Self-Reflection: Identify your core strengths and areas where you feel most engaged.
- ✓ Align with Job Requirements: Relate your strengths to the specific skills or qualities sought by the employer.
- ✓ Provide Concrete Examples: Support your responses with real-world examples that highlight how your strengths contributed to positive outcomes.

Examples of Strength-based Questions with Suggested Answers

Strength-based questions focus on identifying and understanding your key strengths and how they align with the requirements of the role. Here are 10 sample strength-based questions along with recommended answers:

1. Question: "What do you consider to be your strongest professional skill, and how have you applied it to achieve success in your previous roles?"
   Answer: "I consider my strongest skill to be strategic problem-solving. In my previous role, I faced a complex challenge where I was able to analyze the situation, develop a creative solution, and implement it successfully. This resulted in a 20% increase in efficiency for the team."
2. Question: "Can you share an example of a project where you leveraged your leadership skills to motivate a team and achieve exceptional results?"
   Answer: "Leadership is a strength of mine. In a recent project, I took on the role of team lead and motivated the team through clear communication, setting achievable goals, and providing support. This resulted in not only meeting project deadlines but also exceeding client expectations."
3. Question: "What personal attribute do you believe sets you apart from other candidates, and how does it contribute to your success in the workplace?"
   Answer: "I believe my strong sense of adaptability sets me apart. In fast-paced

environments, I've been able to quickly adjust to changing priorities and find innovative solutions. This adaptability has allowed me to thrive in dynamic work situations."

4. Question: "Describe a situation where your communication skills were crucial in achieving a positive outcome. How did you ensure effective communication?"

   Answer: "Effective communication is one of my strengths. In a cross-functional project, I facilitated communication between departments, ensuring everyone was on the same page. This resulted in improved collaboration, minimized misunderstandings, and successful project delivery."

5. Question: "Tell me about a time when you demonstrated exceptional creativity in solving a challenging problem at work."

   Answer: "Creativity is a key strength of mine. In a product launch, I introduced a unique marketing campaign that significantly increased customer engagement. The campaign showcased my ability to think outside the box and contribute to the project's overall success."

6. Question: "How do you approach working in a team, and what unique strengths do you bring to collaborative efforts?"

   Answer: "I thrive in collaborative settings. My ability to actively listen, provide constructive feedback, and leverage each team member's strengths contributes to a positive team dynamic. This collaborative approach has consistently led to successful project outcomes."

7. Question: "What role do you typically play in a team, and how does your approach contribute to the team's overall success?"
   Answer: "I often take on the role of a facilitator in a team. By fostering open communication, encouraging diverse perspectives, and ensuring everyone's contributions are valued, I create an environment where the team can perform at its best."
8. Question: "Can you share an example of a time when you successfully applied your problem-solving skills to overcome a significant obstacle at work?"
   Answer: "Problem-solving is a strength that I actively apply. In a challenging project, I identified a critical bottleneck, devised a solution, and collaborated with the team to implement it. This proactive problem-solving approach led to project success and client satisfaction."
9. Question: "How do you handle tight deadlines and high-pressure situations, and how have these situations showcased your strengths?"
   Answer: "I excel in high-pressure situations. When faced with tight deadlines, I prioritize tasks strategically, maintain composure, and lead the team with a focus on efficiency. This approach has consistently resulted in successful project deliveries, even under challenging circumstances."
10. Question: "What skill or strength are you currently working on improving, and how do you plan to develop it further?"
    Answer: "Continuous improvement is a value I hold. Currently, I am focused on enhancing

my project management skills. I've enrolled in relevant courses, sought mentorship, and actively applied new strategies in my current projects to refine and strengthen this skill."

When responding to strength-based questions, be specific, provide examples from your experiences, and tie your strengths to the needs of the role you're interviewing for. This approach helps the interviewer understand how your unique strengths align with the requirements of the position.

Closing the interview is a crucial phase where candidates can leave a lasting impression. By asking insightful questions that demonstrate genuine interest, avoiding inappropriate queries, and effectively handling strength-based questions, you contribute to the overall positive perception that interviewers have of you.

In summary, this chapter provides guidance on strategically closing the interview by asking relevant questions, steering clear of potential pitfalls, and showcasing your strengths in a positive light. The subsequent chapters will further explore advanced strategies and scenarios to elevate your interview preparedness.

What Next?

Sending Thank-You Notes

The Power of Gratitude: Sending a thank-you note after an interview is a courteous and impactful way to express appreciation for the opportunity, reiterate your interest in the role, and leave a positive lasting impression.

Example:

Dear [Interviewer's Name],

I wanted to express my sincere gratitude for the opportunity to interview for the [Job Title] position at [Company]. It was a pleasure discussing how my skills align with the goals of your team. I am even more enthusiastic about the prospect of contributing to [specific project or initiative] after our conversation.

Thank you again for your time and consideration.
Best regards,
[Your Full Name]

Action Plan:

- ✓ Timeliness: Send the thank-you note within 24 hours of the interview to maintain a timely connection.
- ✓ Personalization: Reference specific aspects of the interview, such as discussions about projects, to make the note more personalized.
- ✓ Professional Tone: Maintain a professional and positive tone throughout the note.

Post-Interview Follow-Up

Proactive Engagement: After the interview, staying engaged and expressing continued interest in the position can set you apart. Following up allows you to reiterate your enthusiasm and inquire about the next steps in the hiring process.

Example:

Dear [Interviewer's Name],

I hope this email finds you well. I wanted to follow up on our recent interview for the [Job Title] position. I am still very interested in the opportunity to contribute to [Company], and I wanted to inquire about the anticipated timeline for the next steps in the hiring process.

Thank you once again for considering my application.
Best regards,
[Your Full Name]

Action Plan:

- ✓ Be Polite and Professional: Craft a concise and polite follow-up email, expressing gratitude and reiterating your interest.
- ✓ Inquire about Timeline: Politely ask about the expected timeline for decisions to demonstrate your continued interest.
- ✓ Express Availability: Mention your availability for any additional information or interviews if needed.

Strategies for Handling Multiple Job Offers

Decision-Making Process: Handling multiple job offers requires a strategic approach to make an informed decision that aligns with your career goals. Consider factors such as job responsibilities, company culture, growth opportunities, and compensation.

Example: Create a comparison chart listing the pros and cons of each job offer, weighing factors such as salary, benefits, career advancement opportunities, and alignment with your long-term goals.

Action Plan:

- ✓ Evaluate Priorities: Identify your priorities in a job, such as work-life balance, growth potential, or company culture.
- ✓ Create a Comparison Chart: Develop a visual aid to compare key factors for each job offer.
- ✓ Seek Advice: Consult with mentors, career advisors, or trusted colleagues for insights and advice.

The post-interview phase is a critical juncture where strategic actions can further solidify your candidacy and guide your decision-making process. Sending thank-you notes and post-interview follow-ups exhibit professionalism and continued interest, while handling multiple job offers requires a systematic approach to ensure alignment with your career objectives.

In summary, this chapter provides guidance on the crucial steps to take after an interview, offering templates and examples for thank-you notes and follow-up emails. Additionally, it explores strategies for navigating the complexities of handling multiple job offers. The subsequent chapters will further explore advanced strategies and scenarios to elevate your interview preparedness.

Conclusion

As we conclude our journey through **'Winning at College Campus Interviews,'** I want to extend my heartfelt congratulations on your commitment to personal and professional growth. The knowledge, strategies, and insights shared within these pages are meant to be more than just tools for acing interviews; they are your companions on the transformative journey from college graduate to successful job candidate.

The world of campus interviews can be both exhilarating and challenging, requiring a unique blend of preparation, confidence, and adaptability. As you reflect on the valuable lessons and practical advice provided in this guide, remember that success is not solely defined by securing a job offer but by the continuous process of learning, evolving, and embracing the opportunities that come your way.

Celebrating Your Journey

Each chapter of this guide has been crafted with the intent of empowering you to navigate the interview landscape with resilience and self-assurance. Whether you are a recent graduate stepping into the professional world for the first time or someone seeking to enhance your interview skills, I hope you found practical and applicable insights that resonate with your unique journey.

As you move forward, keep these key points in mind:

Final Words of Encouragement

Embarking on a career journey can be daunting, but you've demonstrated resilience and commitment by investing time in your preparation. Believe in your abilities, stay confident, and approach each interview as an opportunity to showcase your unique strengths.

Emphasizing the Journey

The transition from college to the professional realm is not just about securing a job; it's a transformative journey of self-discovery and growth. Embrace every experience, whether it's a successful interview or a learning opportunity. Remember that setbacks are stepping stones to success.

A Holistic Approach to Success

Success in campus interviews is not just about delivering impressive answers; it's about presenting the best version of yourself authentically. From understanding the purpose of interviews to sending impactful thank-you notes, each aspect contributes to the holistic tapestry of your interview success.

Embracing Continuous Learning

The professional journey is dynamic and ever-evolving. As you step into the corporate world, remember the importance of continuous learning. Stay curious, adapt to change, and view each interview as an opportunity not only to showcase your skills but to learn more about yourself and your professional aspirations.

Moving Forward with Confidence

As you move forward in your career, carry the confidence instilled by your preparation and the lessons learned from each interview. Your ability to navigate the complexities of the interview process reflects not only your qualifications but also your resilience and determination.

In closing, may the knowledge gained from this guide be a source of inspiration and empowerment as you embark on the next phase of your career. May you face each interview with confidence, authenticity, and a mindset of continuous improvement. Your success is not just a destination but a journey of self-discovery and professional accomplishment.

Wishing you all the best in your future interviews and may you continue to keep soaring higher!

About the Author 'GERARD ASSEY'

Gerard Assey is a Graduate in Economics, a PGD in Management (HRD) and holds a Doctorate in Leadership. Gerard holds several International Qualifications in Sales, Debt Collection, Training & Teaching, and is a 'Fellow' of the prestigious 'Institute of Sales & Marketing Management'-UK, a Certified NLP Practitioner, a 'Certified Trainer', an 'Accredited Management Teacher-Behavioral Sciences', a 'Certified Competency Facilitator', a 'Certified Management Consultant'- (the International credentials of a professional management consultant, awarded in accordance with global standards of the ICMCI); and a Certification from the University of Michigan in 'Successful Negotiation: Essential Strategies and Skills'

He is also a Member of the 'National Association of Sales Professionals' backed with several years experience in varied industries, both in India and Overseas. He also holds an 'Etiquette Consultant' Certification from the USA (by Sue Fox, Author of Best Seller: 'Business Etiquette for Dummies'. She has trained some of the top celebrities' world over). He was also a recipient of a scholarship for extensive training in Japan on 'Corporate Management for India'.

Gerard Assey is 'Founder & Chief Corporate Trainer' of the Group: '**Citius, Altius, Fortius Unlimited**'- an organization that **celebrated 20 years of Glorious**

Service in 2021, focusing on 3 Core Competencies: **People. Performance. Profit**; in functional areas of Sales & Marketing, HR & Organizational Development, covering Recruitment, Training & Consultancy!

Having managed organizations with large Sales Forces in India & Overseas, his specialization cover extensive areas of Sales Training (All levels - Presentation, Negotiation, Key/ Strategic Accounts Management & Managerial Skills for all sectors), Bid Proposal/ Capture Planning/ Management Trainings, Retail Sales, Customer Service & Customer Retention Programs, Training for Prevention & Collection of Debt, Self & Personal Development Programs (Time Management, Teamwork & Team Building, Business Etiquette & Personal Grooming, Leadership & Managerial Skills, People Management Skills, Train-the-Trainer etc), including preparation of Custom-designed Business Manuals for Internal (HR, Induction, and Sales etc) & External use (Instruction, User Manuals).

Gerard has successfully conducted over 6050 Trainings & Workshops (as of Jan '24) all across India, Middle East, Africa, Europe & S.E. Asia. Besides public programs conducted regularly, both in India & Overseas, he has some of the top names as clients whom he services from Single Owners to large Public & Government undertakings, covering all sectors, for their in-house needs.

His website: www.CollectionSkills.com is the only one in this part of the world to be featured in the 'Collections & Credit Risk Magazine-USA' under 'Who's Who in Training' and ranks TOP, along with other websites listed below on most search engines.

Gerard is author of 104 books already (Jan 2024)

A few of our business related books:

1. Bite-sized Bits on Commonsense Management
2. Heart to Heart on Life's Principles'
3. How to become a Successful Manager
4. The Sales Professionals' Master Workbook of S.Y.S.T.E.M.S
5. The Professional Business Email Etiquette Handbook & Guide
6. The Professional Business Video-Conferencing Etiquette Handbook & Guide
7. Professional Presentation Skills
8. Exceptional Customer Service
9. Professional Tele-Marketing Skills
10. Professional Debt Collection Skills
11. The G.R.E.A.T. Sales & Service Workbook
12. Sales Training Advantage for Results (*The Ultimate Sales Training Manual to enable you stand out as a S.T.A.R.*)
13. CEO Daily Planner & Organizer
14. The Sales Professionals' Master Daily Planner
15. The Professional Debt Collector's Master Daily Planner
16. My Daily Planner & Organizer
17. MY EMERGENCY INFORMATION RECORD (Family Emergency & Peace of Mind Planner)
18. The Ultimate Therapist & Counselors Planner and Organizer
19. Building an Ethical Workplace
20. Managing Relationships at Work
21. Managing Business Meetings Effectively
22. Effective Delegation Skills
23. Goal Setting for Success
24. B2B Selling by Email
25. Professional Business Etiquette & Grooming
26. Dining Etiquette & Table Manners
27. Effective Networking Skills
28. Grooming, Etiquette & Manners for Teens, Young Adults & Future Leaders
29. Inter-Personal Skills
30. Get Ready, Get Hired!
31. Selling in a Recession
32. Effective Receivables Management in an Economic Downturn!
33. Real Estate & Property Sales Training
34. Credit Sales & Accounts Receivable Management
35. Selling Skills for Real Estate & Property Advisors
36. Take G.R.E.A.T. C.A.R.E!
37. Spa, Salon & Health Club Selling Skills
38. Selling Travel, Holiday & MICE Services
39. Selling Skills for Spa's, Salons & Health Clubs

40. Retailing in Salons & Spas
41. Selling Holiday, Vacation, Tours & Packages
42. The Power of Sales Referrals
43. Selling Luxury
44. Technical Selling Skills
45. Financial Advisors Sales Training
46. Dealing with Burnout at Work Monopolize Your Markets
47. Selling to Affluent Customers
48. Growing up with Grace
49. Financial Selling Skills
50. *The Effective Manager's Guide: Key Skills to Thrive*
51. From Aspiring to Inspiring: A Guide for New Managers on the Rise
52. The Power of Focus
53. Selling with Integrity: Sell Like Jesus The Perfect Role Model!
54. 31 Habits of Champions: Your 31-Day Journey to Greatness
55. Rejecting Grasshopper Talk: From Grasshopper to Giant-Killer-*Defeating Giants Daily!*
56. Navigate the AI-Powered Future of Bid & Proposals: Up-Skill to Stay Relevant with Alternative Career Paths & Opportunities
57. Hiring Sales Winners
58. Present with Impact
59. Success Unlocked: *Breaking Free from Habits that Hold You Back*
60. Complaints to Cheers, Feedback to Gold: Mastering Complaints Management
61. Thriving Together: *Cultivating Diversity, Equity, and Inclusion*
62. Coaching Skills for Sales Managers
63. Soaring to Success in Business & Leadership: Swifter, Higher, Stronger!
64. From Classroom to Podium: A Student's Guide to Powerful Public Speaking & Presentation Skills
65. Developing Self-Discipline
66. The CEO's 31-Day Power Plan: Unlocking Success through Essential Traits
67. Credibility Matters
68. A Winning Attitude
69. Bid & Proposal Management Using AI
70. Sales Forecasting: A Practical & Proven Guide to Strategic Sales Forecasting
71. Winning at College Campus Interviews

Besides regularly contributing to business & trade journals, including international ones such as the 'Creative Training Techniques' and the 'Sales News' of the U.S.A, He is also a member of several prestigious bodies & trade associations, having participated in many Conferences & Workshops in India & Overseas.

Prior to his last assignment of leading & managing a large MNC as head, Gerard had a 3-year stint in the Middle East as a Consultant with a leading British Consultancy Firm.

As the past 'Official Country Representative' for the International Business Award- 'THE STEVIES'-(the business world's own Oscar) for about 4 years- he ensured a few Indian companies that qualify for the same every year!

Gerard can be contacted at:
Email: training@Sales-Training.in,training@CollectionSkills.com
Websites:

www.Sales-Training.in
www.EtiquetteWorks.in
www.CollectionSkills.com
www.RetailSalesTraining.in
www.SalesTrainingIndia.com
www.ManualPreparation.com
www.TrainingWithPuppets.com
www.FirstContactAcademy.com
www.SalesAndMarketingRecruiter.com

Our TRAININGS that can help your team

- ✓ **Sales Effectiveness**: Selling Skills for any Sector: Service/ Logistics/ FMCG Realty/ Insurance & Finance/ Media/ SPA's, Health Clubs & Salons/ Key Account Management, Effective Negotiation Skills/ Bid & Proposal Management Skills/ Retail Sales Training: Any Sector (Auto, Jewelry, Clothing, Luxury etc)
- ✓ **Customer Service Skills**-Complaints Handling & Customer Retention
- ✓ **Debt Prevention & Collection Skills**
- ✓ **Etiquette & Grooming**
- ✓ **Leadership & Managerial Skills**
- ✓ **Self & Personal Development Skills**: Presentation Skills/ Effective Communication Skills/Business Proposal Writing Skills/ Problem Solving & Decision Making Skills/ Empowering Secretaries-The perfect PA! (For Secretaries & PA's)/ Effective Time Management/ Teamwork & Teambuilding/ P.R.I.D.E- **P**ersonal **R**esponsibility **I**n **D**elivering **E**xcellence

www.ingramcontent.com/pod-product-compliance
Lightning Source LLC
LaVergne TN
LVHW010104170826
845678LV00012B/2236

* 9 7 8 8 1 9 6 7 2 0 2 7 8 *